Climate Change Resiliency Planning Into Businesses in the Cayman Islands

Dr. the Hon. Linford A. Pierson, OBE, JP

Dedication

This book is dedicated to God for His guidance and wisdom; to my beloved wife, Sharon, for her unwavering support and inspiration; and to the resilient people of the Cayman Islands, whose strength and courage in the face of climate change challenges continue to serve as an example of dedication and perseverance.

Preface

The Cayman Islands, renowned for their pristine beaches, vibrant marine life, and unique cultural heritage, stand as a testament to the beauty and fragility of our natural world. However, as climate change accelerates, this idyllic archipelago finds itself on the front lines of a global crisis that threatens not only its environment but also the very way of life of its people. The impetus for writing this book comes from a profound sense of urgency and responsibility.

The effects of climate change are no longer distant predictions; they are being felt today. Sea level rise, more frequent and intense hurricanes, and shifting weather patterns are realities that the Cayman Islands must face head-on. The need for comprehensive and effective resiliency planning has never been more critical. A significant portion of the research for this book was drawn from my dissertation submitted in partial fulfillment of the degree of Master of Business Administration (MBA).

This book aims to provide a thorough examination of the challenges posed by climate change to the Cayman Islands and to explore the strategies that can be employed to build resilience. Drawing on the latest scientific research, case studies from other vulnerable regions, and insights from local experts, this work is designed to be a practical guide for policymakers, planners, and the community at large.

Writing this book has been both a challenging and enlightening journey. The complexity of the issues at hand, coupled with the diverse perspectives from stakeholders across the Islands, underscored the importance of a holistic approach to climate change resiliency. Every chapter of this book reflects a commitment to understanding and addressing these challenges in a way that is sustainable, equitable, and informed by the best available knowledge.

As you read through these pages, you will encounter discussions on the physical vulnerabilities of the Islands, the socio-economic impacts of climate change, and the critical role that local communities play in fostering resilience. You will also find practical recommendations for building infrastructure that can withstand extreme weather events, preserving the Islands' natural resources, and ensuring that the Cayman Islands remain a thriving and livable place for generations to come.

This book is not just a compilation of research and strategies—it is a call to action. The decisions we make today will have an impact on the future of the Cayman Islands. By embracing a forward-thinking and resilient approach to planning, we can protect this precious environment and the livelihoods of those who call it home.

I am deeply grateful to the ten participants who were interviewed for this study and other individuals who contributed their time, knowledge, and passion to this project. Their insights have been invaluable in shaping the content and direction of this book. I hope that this work will serve as a valuable resource for those dedicated to safeguarding the Cayman Islands against the impacts of climate change.

With this preface, I invite you to join me on this exploration of climate change resiliency planning in the

Cayman Islands. Together, let us work towards a future where the natural beauty and cultural richness of these Islands are preserved for all who live here and for those who will follow.

About the Author

Dr. the Hon. Linford A. Pierson, OBE, JP, PhD (Educ. Psychol.), Doctor of Public Service (h.c.), LLM, MBA, MAPPC, FCCA, is an indigenous Caymanian who has served in various positions in the public and private sectors of the Cayman Islands, briefly outlined hereunder:

- Dr. Pierson served in the Civil Service for 16 years, attaining the position of Permanent Secretary (re-designated Chief Officer). During this period, he spent four years in London, UK, where he obtained his professional accounting designation, becoming the first native-born Caymanian to qualify as a professional accountant from the Association of Chartered Certified Accountants (ACCA) in 1978. He was elevated to Fellow of the Association of Chartered Certified Accountants (FCCA) in 1983. In 2016, Dr. Pierson was awarded pioneer recognition by the Cayman Islands Institute of Professional Accountants for being the first native-born Caymanian to qualify as a professional accountant.

- Following his Civil Service career, Dr Pierson held various positions in the private sector in the early 1980s, including serving as the local partner of the then-Canadian accounting firm Thorne Riddell (KPMG). This was followed by more than 16 years as an elected member of the Legislative Assembly/Parliament. During his political career, he served as a Minister of Government and later as Speaker of the Legislative Assembly/Parliament until his retirement in May 2005.

- In 2002, Dr. Pierson was honored by the Government of the Cayman Islands with the naming of the 'Linford Pierson Highway' in recognition of his contribution to the development of roads throughout the Cayman Islands—Grand Cayman, Cayman Brac, and Little Cayman.

- The title of Honorable ('Hon.') in perpetuity was bestowed on Dr. Pierson in 2012 by the Government of the Cayman Islands. This recognition is legally granted to individuals who have held the posts of (i) Premier, (ii) Leader of Government Business, and (iii) Speaker of the Legislative Assembly/Parliament. Dr. Pierson is a former Speaker of the Legislative Assembly/Parliament.

- Following his retirement, Dr. Pierson pursued his academic goals, as follows:

   o A Master of Arts degree in Pastoral Psychology and Counselling (MAPPC) from St. Stephen's College, Alberta, Canada, in 2008;

   o A PhD in Educational Psychology from Walden University, USA in 2012;

   o An LLM in International Commercial Law (with distinction) from the University of Salford, UK in 2022; and

   o An MBA (with merit) from the University of Cumbria, UK in 2024.

- In 2021, Dr. Pierson was honored by his alma mater, Northern Caribbean University (NCU), with the award of

Doctor of Public Service (Honoris Causa) in recognition of his public service to the Cayman Islands.

- Since 2019, Dr. Pierson has been qualified as an APMG Certified Public-Private Partnership (PPP) Professional.

- In addition to the foregoing, Dr. Pierson has served on several Boards in the public and private sectors and has been active in community service, including as a Rotarian for 48 years (1968-2016).

- Dr. Pierson has published his autobiography, titled: *Empowered by Faith - A Lifelong Journey with Jesus Christ.* In addition to this book on *Climate Change Resiliency Planning into Businesses in the Cayman Islands*, he has also written the following two books:

  1. *Working Memory Training to Improve School Preparedness of Children with Attention-Deficit/Hyperactivity Disorder (ADHD)*, based on his PhD dissertation in Educational Psychology; and

  2. *A Critical Assessment of the Relationship between Intellectual Property Law and Competition Law in the Era of Artificial Intelligence*, based on his LLM dissertation in International Commercial Law.

Abstract

The research study for this book conducts a critical analysis of the perceived factors influencing the successful integration of climate change resiliency planning into businesses in the Cayman Islands. Small Island Developing States (SIDS), such as the Cayman Islands, face increased vulnerability to climate change impacts, including hurricanes, sea level rise, flooding, storm surges, and other extreme weather events, which pose significant risks to the economic stability and sustainability of these Islands.

Through qualitative interviews with ten key stakeholders across various sectors of the Cayman Islands, including tourism, financial services, and real estate, this research identifies and evaluates the critical factors that contribute to—or hinder—the adoption of effective resilience strategies. The findings reveal that strong Government support and regulatory frameworks are key to encouraging the implementation of resilience measures. Financial constraints, however, remain a significant challenge, particularly for small businesses. The study highlights the importance of community engagement and collaboration, innovative adaptation strategies, and the critical role of tourism in the economy, which serves as both a strength and a weakness.

By comparing these insights with existing literature and theoretical frameworks, the book emphasizes the necessity of targeted policy interventions, financial incentives, and capacity-building initiatives to foster a resilient business environment. The research contributes to a deeper understanding of the unique challenges and opportunities faced by businesses in the Cayman Islands. It provides actionable recommendations for policymakers and business leaders to emulate and enhance climate change resilience. This book offers practical guidance for the development, sustainability, and resilient economic future of the Cayman Islands.

Keywords: Climate Change, Planning Resiliency, Renewables, SIDS, GHG

Abbreviations

Acronym	Full Name
AI	Artificial Intelligence
AOSIS	Alliance of Small Island States
BRI	Building Resilience Intervention
CCRA	Climate Change Risk Assessment
CCRIF	Caribbean Catastrophe Risk Insurance Facility
CDC	Centers for Disease Control and Prevention
CDEMA	Caribbean Disaster Emergency Management Agency
CICCP	Cayman Islands Climate Change Policy
CIG	Cayman Islands Government
COP	Conference of the Parties
EIA	Energy Information Administration

EPA	Environmental Protection Agency
EVs	Electric Vehicles
GDP	Gross Domestic Product
GDPR	General Data Protection Regulation
GHG	Greenhouse Gases
GIS	Geographic Information System
HMCI	Hazard Management Cayman Islands
IEA	International Energy Agency
IPCC	Intergovernmental Panel on Climate Change
ISO	International Organization for Standardization
JESIP	Joint Emergency Service Interoperability Programme
MS	Member States [of the United Nations]
NEP	National Energy Policy

NEPA	National Environmental Policy Act
NHC	National Hurricane Center
NOAA	National Oceanic Atmospheric Administration
PA	Paris Agreement
PM2.5	Particulate Matter less than 2.5 micrometers
PPPs	Private-Public-Partnerships
PV	Photovoltaics
SDGs	Sustainable Development Goals
SIDS	Small Island Developing States
UKOTA	United Kingdom Overseas Territories Association
UNCED	United Nations Conference on Environment and Development
UNDP	United Nations Development Programme

UNECLAC	United Nations Economic Commission for Latin America and the Caribbean
UNEP	United Nations Environmental Programme
UNESCO	United Nations Education, Scientific and Cultural Organization
UNFCCC	United Nations Framework Convention on Climate Change
WHO	World Health Organization
WMO	World Meteorological Organization

Contents

Chapter 1: Introduction

1.1 Purpose and Scope

The factors that influence the successful implementation of climate change resiliency planning into businesses in the Cayman Islands can be attributed to the country's ability to quickly recover from disruptions caused by force majeure events, including perennial hurricanes and pandemics such as COVID-19. For example, in a total population of approximately 43,000 (2004), the economic impact on the Cayman Islands in 2004 from Hurricane Ivan, a category 5 hurricane on the Saffir-Simpson scale, was estimated by the United Nations Economic Commission for Latin America and the Caribbean (UNECLAC) to be USD 3.4 billion (Government of the Cayman Islands, 2010). Moreover, the economic damage to the Cayman Islands resulting from the COVID-19 pandemic, with a population of approximately 66,000 (2020), was estimated at USD 56.95 million (Panadés-Estruch, 2021).

In keeping with the post-Ivan recommendations and sound international strategies, the Government established the Hazard Management Cayman Islands (HMCI) office, which became operational in 2008, to assume responsibilities relating to all hazards that pose a threat to the Cayman Islands. Despite the relatively small population of the Cayman Islands during these two major disasters, the exceptional response in successfully coping with these catastrophes is remarkable and indicative of the strong resiliency of businesses and environmental sustainability extant within the Cayman Islands.

The Cayman Islands are one of 57 countries designated by the United Nations Conference on Environment and Development (UNCED) as Small Island Developing States (SIDS). Of this number, 39 are designated as States, and 18 (including the Cayman Islands) are designated Associate Members of the United Nations Regional Commissions (UNESCO, 1992).

The Cayman Islands consist of three small, low-lying islands (Grand Cayman, Cayman Brac, and Little Cayman) situated about 180 miles (290km) northwest of Jamaica. The shortest distance south (by airline) between Miami, Florida, and the Cayman Islands is 433.23 miles (697.22 km) (Britannica, 2024). The authors also stated that the Cayman Islands are located "on the boundary between two tectonic plates, one moving eastward and one moving westward; tremors resulting from the movements of the plates are sometimes recorded."

According to Panadés-Estruch (2021), the economy is supported by banking, tourism, real estate sales and development, and other services. The implementation of climate change resiliency into businesses in the Cayman Islands involves a series of strategic, operational, and infrastructural adaptations aimed at enabling businesses to withstand and quickly recover from the damages caused by the negative impacts of climate change (Ministry of Sustainability & Climate Resiliency, 2023).

Given the vulnerability of SIDS, such as the Cayman Islands, the relevant research question is: What perceived factors can successfully integrate climate change resiliency planning into businesses in the Cayman Islands? To answer

2

this question, it is important to assess the vulnerabilities of the Cayman Islands to extreme weather events such as hurricanes, sea level rise, flooding, and other force majeure climate-related conditions.

According to Johnston and Cooper (2022), the Cayman Islands are susceptible to the negative impacts of climate change, and the mitigation and adaptation of effective strategies are vital to developing climate change resiliency and achieving sustainable development goals. The authors further stated that resilience planning is multifaceted and includes various types of mitigating sources, including (i) solar energy, (ii) wind energy, (iii) geothermal energy, (iv) nuclear energy, (v) ocean thermal energy conversion, and (vi) artificial intelligence. Solar energy is the most popular renewable energy source used in the Cayman Islands, no doubt because the Caribbean is ideal for the high levels of sunlight available.

Camarinhas (2020) posited that, with one of the highest disaster rates in the world, the Caribbean region requires disaster risk reduction to combat the problem of the perennial vulnerabilities experienced by SIDS, such as the Cayman Islands. Planning resilience must, therefore, consider the implementation of various methods to tackle climate change. To mitigate the impacts, it is essential to include adaptation of protective infrastructure into business operations and government policies.

Pinnegar *et al.* (2022) stated in their *Cayman Islands Climate Change Evidence Report* that the *Cayman Islands Climate Change Policy (2011)* was designed to support the transformation to a "climate-resilient, low-carbon economy." This transformation included implementing processes to enhance the resilience of current critical infrastructure, as well as constructing new infrastructure facilities in compliance with government building codes. Additionally, the policy aimed to improve the resilience and "natural adaptive capacity of terrestrial, marine and coastal biodiversity and ecosystems" while also developing a sustainable tourism industry, including the enhancement of resilience by strengthening the structural integrity of buildings and business operations in the Cayman Islands (Pinnegar *et al.*, 2022). Given the geographical and economic situation of the Cayman Islands, the development of resilience for businesses requires a range of backup systems to ensure an uninterrupted supply of goods and services.

As regards the *Cayman Islands Climate Change Risk Assessment (CCRA)*, Reid (2023) commented that the Cayman Islands face imminent threats posed by climate change and further stated that "the final evidence report of the Climate Change Risk Assessment identifies, scores and ranks, 50 risks related to biodiversity and habitats, the economy, and society in the Cayman Islands". The key findings of the risk report analyzed important physical climate change drivers and impacts, including changes in storms, cyclones, winds, waves, and storm surges; sea level rise; increasing air and sea temperatures; changes in ocean salinity; ocean acidification; and changes to rainfall patterns (Reid, 2023).

While the need to address climate change is widely accepted, the problem that the research explores is the perceived gap in the general strategic integration of resilience planning into businesses in the Cayman Islands. The *2023-2040 Cayman Islands Climate Change Policy (CICCP)* aims to deliver a robust strategy to tackle the adverse effects of climate change on the economy, with the view to achieving a "Low Carbon-Resilient Economy" (Ministry of Sustainability & Climate Resiliency, 2023). The CICCP encapsulates in its vision statement provision for "a climate-resilient Cayman Islands that promotes and sustains vibrant communities, a thriving natural environment, and a robust economy, where people can live their best lives now and for future generations."

The Cayman Islands National Energy Policy (NEP) (2023-2050) focuses on renewable energy. The NEP targets (i) 100% renewable energy by 2050 and (ii) 100% electric vehicles by 2050 (Ministry of Sustainability & Climate Resiliency, 2023). In 2021, the Cayman Islands Government, in partnership with the UK Centre for Ecology and Hydrology, identified the need for the Cayman Islands to increase its climate resiliency, as two of the three Islands have low-lying topographies (Johnston and Cooper, 2022).

Tompkins, Lemos, and Boyd (2008) stated that "the lesson from the Cayman Islands study is that integrated, learning-based management systems, with widespread buy-in and support, can deliver long-term risk reduction benefits. "On the question of mitigation, adaptation, and resilience, Mewes (2018) stated that mitigation could assist in minimizing the negative impacts of climate change as adaptation assists in preparing for negative climate change, and resilience assists in developing a smooth and timely recovery from negative impacts of climate change events. Mewes further stated that climate change resilience can be facilitated by "an early warning system that predicts and monitors hazardous events, including extreme weather events."

1.2 Aim and Objectives

The aim of the study is to critically analyze the perceived barriers to the successful integration of resiliency planning into businesses in the Cayman Islands. The aim is supported by the following objectives:

- To explore current international trends for resiliency planning and determine an evaluation of resilience in businesses in the Cayman Islands;

- To gather a range of perspectives from key stakeholders in the Cayman Islands and identify any perceived barriers to attaining CICCP's vision relating to the integration of climate change resilience into business strategies;

- To analyze underlying factors for, or barriers against, successful implementation of resiliency programs by critically assessing the impact of local and international policies relating to resiliency in businesses in the Cayman Islands;

- To assess the current state of climate resiliency planning integrated into business practices in the Cayman Islands to determine any existing gaps and strengths;

- To derive conclusions and, based on the analysis, propose actionable recommendations for the future practice of businesses in the Cayman Islands to successfully integrate resiliency into their operations.

Chapter 2: Literature Review

2.1 Introduction to the Literature Review

The literature review is based on the following research question: What perceived factors can successfully integrate climate change resiliency planning into businesses in the Cayman Islands? It is crucial to comprehensively address climate change challenges globally as well as in the Cayman Islands, as countries such as China, the United States of America, the European Union, India, Russia, and Japan contribute 99% of global GHG emissions, compared to SIDS, such as the Cayman Islands, which contribute less than 1% of the world's GHG emissions (Ortega-Ruiz *et al.*, 2022).

In this connection, a relevant question that arose in COP28 (2023) was: Should India and China benefit from the climate damage fund? In response to this question, Khadka (2023) stated that China, the United States of America, and India are the three highest global emitters of GHG. Together with other large global emitters, they should make significant cuts in GHG emissions and therefore be the biggest contributors to the "Loss and Damage Fund for Developing Countries." This fund was established by the UN Climate Change Conference 2022 (COP27) in Egypt "to create a fund that will help low-income developing countries offset the damage from natural disasters caused by climate change" (UNDP, 2024).

As a result of the increase in the frequency and intensity of the negative impacts of climate change, vulnerable countries such as the Cayman Islands must undertake a critical analysis

7

of the perceived factors for the successful integration of climate change resiliency planning. The insightful contributions made by Tompkins and Hurlston (2005) on natural hazards and climate change, and by Tompkins, Hurlston, and Poortinga (2009) on disaster resilience, provided the basis for understanding that disaster resilience is the ability of a system, community, or society exposed to hazards to resist, absorb, accommodate and recover from the effects of those hazards in a timely and efficient manner. Also, the lessons learned in disaster resilience can equally apply to natural hazards and climate change. This research examines the effects of renewables and other climate change resiliency planning on businesses in the Cayman Islands and globally.

The background of this research provided primary data through interviews and secondary data from scientific literature on the global impacts of climate change, including SIDS with comparable vulnerabilities to the Cayman Islands. These data support the view that the Cayman Islands are susceptible to the adverse effects of climate change. Climate change has been proven to pose a significant challenge to social, developmental, and environmental sustainability (Johnston and Cooper, 2022). According to Camarinhas (2020), the Caribbean region has one of the highest climate change disaster rates in the world. The author further stated that disaster risk reduction is essential to combat the perennial vulnerabilities experienced by SIDS, such as the Cayman Islands, and that resilience planning should consider the implementation of various methods to tackle climate change within the Caribbean area.

Grant *et al.* (2023) stated that the Caribbean region is susceptible to the common problem of "vulnerability and risk of disappearing if the damages of climate change and global warming are not addressed collectively and urgently." The authors also commented that although various international indices and measuring tools are employed to aggregate data and examine risks resulting from climate change, "no index is explicitly developed for the Caribbean." The examination of research on SIDS, such as the Cayman Islands, provides a comparative analysis of challenges and opportunities in climate change resiliency and also lays the groundwork for the further study of perceived factors for the successful integration of climate change resiliency into businesses in the Cayman Islands. Section 2.2 of this Chapter considers various aspects for the successful integration of climate change resiliency planning into businesses in the Cayman Islands.

2.2 Review of Factors Which Determine the Successful Integration of Climate Change Resiliency Planning into Businesses in the Cayman Islands

2.2.1 Reduction in GHG Emissions

Largely developed and developing countries, which emit 99% of GHG, are key to the world's reduction of GHG. However, it is incumbent on SIDS, such as the Cayman Islands, which are on the front lines of extreme weather events, to adopt climate change policies, including renewable energy, such as solar energy, to avoid future costs associated with GHG. The integration of renewable energy into climate change resiliency planning is therefore crucial for sustainable development, as are other GHG reduction methods.

Coiante and Barra (1996) argued that the main advantage of renewables is their very low emission of GHG compared to fossil fuel energy. However, the disadvantages of renewables, such as solar energy, include their unreliability at night and during cloudy weather in the absence of energy storage solutions (such as batteries), as well as the substantial amount of land space required for large-scale consumption. Dalby (2020) examined the question of environmental security as it relates to climate change and observed that although the Paris Agreement highlighted the importance of addressing climate change, efforts to securitize climate change have not become a priority "for most states nor for the United Nations" despite numerous attempts to deal with this matter.

Although the Paris Agreement (PA) attempted to gain global support for climate change, Raiser *et al.* (2020) have questioned the effectiveness of the Agreement in achieving its targets. The authors further stated that "despite the diplomatic success of 195 member states (MS) agreeing on such a consequential and legally binding text, the efficacy of the PA remains under intense scrutiny." Regarding social science perspectives on drivers and responses to global climate change, Jorgenson *et al.* (2018) asserted that humans were the major drivers of carbon emissions, caused directly or indirectly, with larger nations being the biggest offenders. According to Turrentine (2022), the key to addressing climate change lies in the transition from fossil fuels to clean energy such as solar energy, which "currently accounts for just under 3 percent of the electricity generated in the United States—enough to power 18 million homes—but is growing at a faster rate than any other source. By 2035, it could account for as much as 40%."

2.2.2 Various Methods for Asset Securitization

Based on a Geographic Information System (GIS) approach to interpret geographic data in the assessment of hurricane hazards and vulnerability in the Cayman Islands, in the interest of assets securitization, Taramelli, Valentini, and Sterlacchini (2014) identified various elements of critical facilities at risk, such as the seaport and airport, which were described as being potentially subject to severe damage from strong winds and storm surges. The authors also emphasized the need for the Cayman Islands to obtain "ready-to-use GIS-based vulnerability methodologies for risk assessment."

Regarding hurricane preparedness, Tompkins (2005) emphasized the need for the Cayman Islands Government to encourage the participation of individuals as well as private sector businesses. On adaptations to hurricanes in the Mexican Caribbean, Manuel-Navarrete, Pelling, and Redclift (2010) stated that, despite established adaptation plans, there is significant opposition between the controlling influence of mass tourism and "the ostensible embracing of an alternative vision based on ecological modernization."

In regard to challenges relating to small islands and climate change, Johnston and Cooper (2022) posited that small islands are susceptible to the negative impacts of climate change and that the implementation of essential adaptation strategies is urgently needed. Robinson (2015) asserted that although SIDS are most vulnerable to the effects of climate change, there is "little information in the academic literature about how SIDS are adapting to climate change across multiple countries and geographic regions."

Adger *et al.* (2011) examined whether specific strategic reactions to climate change could effectively undermine long-term resilience in free enterprise systems. In their discussion on the short-term and long-term effectiveness of the Paris Agreement, Bang, Hovi, and Skodvin (2016) opined that, as in the case of the 1997 Kyoto Protocol, which was rejected by China, Australia, and the United States of America, the 2015 Paris Agreement could suffer a similar fate of the non-binding agreement. They noted that "deep political polarization continues to represent a significant barrier to U.S. leadership on climate change."

Commentary by Abbasi, Premalatha, and Abbasi (2010) suggested that it is necessary to significantly decrease dependence on fossil fuel energy before renewables can have any significant effect on reducing GHG emissions. Karakosta *et al.* (2013) also discussed the pros and cons of "renewable energy and nuclear power toward sustainability." They stated that both renewable energy and nuclear energy provide a low footprint of GHG. However, the downside of nuclear energy is the inherent danger of "weapons proliferation, safety, waste handling, and high cost as well as public acceptance." Similar concerns were raised by Muellner *et al.* (2021), who questioned whether nuclear energy is the solution to climate change and averred that the advantages of atomic energy are limited when compared to the disadvantages of exposure to "catastrophic accidents, proliferation, and radioactive waste."

Despite the position taken by Shellenberger (2017) in his statement that "renewables can't save the planet—but uranium can," he noted that in 2014, 78% of participants in a global survey agreed with the statement that "In the future renewable energy sources will be able to fully replace fossil fuels." In this connection, Ghoneem (2016) questioned why planning for climate change matters. While there are various commentaries on the question of climate change, according to the United Nations Environmental Programme (UNEP, 2007), in the interest of the protection of a country's population, most responsible countries balance "social, economic, and environmental needs." As regards planning the resilient city, with the understanding that resilient cities can absorb, recover, and prepare for unforeseen occurrences, resilient cities will promote sustainable development through the processes of mitigation, adaptation, and resiliency planning (Jabareen, 2013). With respect to resilient communities, Alameldeen and Cakan (2021) used as an example the resettlement of refugees in developed countries to allow them a fresh start in life.

2.2.3 Inequities of Climate Change Relative to SIDS

The fundamental dilemma experienced by SIDS, such as the Cayman Islands, is that while the emission of GHG emitted by SIDS is less than 1% of global emissions, they are "worst affected by changing climatic conditions" (Betzold, 2015). The author further stated that SIDS are among the first to adapt to climate change and, as such, can serve as positive models to larger countries. In the article by Thomas *et al.* (2020) regarding the risk to SIDS by climate change, the United Nations Framework Convention on Climate Change (UNFCCC) recognizes them as a special group. Also, the Alliance of Small Island States (AOSIS) has been a strong negotiating group in the UNFCCC. The AOSIS '1.5°C to Stay Alive' campaign was primarily responsible for the inclusion of

13

the global temperature goal in the 2015 Paris Agreement and also supported the request for the Intergovernmental Panel on Climate Change (IPCC) to produce a special report on the implications of 1.5°C of global warming. Attard *et al.* (2021) recommended long-term strategies to allow governments to establish appropriate planning for a resilient, decarbonized future that is compatible with limiting warming to 1.5 °C.

In the context of the Cayman Islands, the main policy goal is the phasing out of fossil fuel energy to be replaced by renewable energy by 2050 (Ministry of Sustainability & Climate Resiliency, 2023).

The views of Weir and Kumar (2020) relating to the enhancement of resilience by renewable energy support the position taken by the Ministry of Sustainability & Climate Resiliency (2023). As stated by the authors, "Renewable energy, coupled with improved energy efficiency, can enhance island resilience to natural hazards and economic shocks." In answering the question: "Does renewable energy reduce per capita carbon emissions and per capita ecological footprint?" based on empirical evidence obtained from 130 countries, Li, Wang, and Li (2023) concluded that "an increase in renewable energy consumption has a significant inhibitory effect on the growth of ecological footprint," and that a significant method to cut GHG directly is by using renewables.

In support of renewable energy, Sims (2004) asserted that an "acceptable future world, with minimum cost needed for adaptation resulting from climate change, will, *inter alia*, require the rapid uptake of renewables to displace fossil fuels." Sims also opined that there would be a significant increase in businesses "as the world decarbonizes and moves into the Renewable Energy Era." In their article on the importance of renewable energy, Koeva, Kutkarska, and Zinoviev (2023) argued that renewable energy is crucial in the transitional development of green energy and key to EU countries becoming less dependent on fossil fuel energy, "and the dependence on Russian imported fuel." The possibilities of large countries complying with GHG reductions still hang in the balance, thus continuing the exposure of SIDS, such as the Cayman Islands, to the inequities of climate change.

2.2.4 Geostrategic Factors Relating to Global Warming

The commentary by Nurse and Moore (2005) regarding the urgency of adaptation of SIDS to global climate change is pertinent to the vulnerability of SIDS. Further, the primarily held belief that SIDS, such as the Cayman Islands, are remote, beautiful places that are unaffected by climate change occurrences in the rest of the world is a fallacy. The views expressed by Jayaram (2013) regarding the case study of the Indo-Maldivian Island nation are equally applicable to other SIDS, including the Cayman Islands. The uninhabitability resulting from flooding, sea level rise, and lack of freshwater is a reality common to all SIDS. The geographical location of a state plays a vital role in determining its geopolitics; geostrategy is defined as "the combination of geopolitical and strategic factors characterizing a particular geographic region" (Merriam-Webster Dictionary). According to Behnassi (2014), "global warming, as a new geostrategic issue, is putting international relations under pressure with a potential to affect government structures." Pflüger (2020) stated that climate change jeopardizes world peace as a result of geopolitical problems arising from migration and food and water shortages and is thus a general threat to environmental sustainability.

On the question of the taxonomy and metrics relative to the adaptation to climate change, Boutang *et al.* (2020) acknowledged that adaptation to climate change is a continual challenge for governments and businesses and suggested that organizations should use appropriate measures to assess their adaptation resiliency to climate change effectively. Rashidi-Sabet, Madhavaram, and Parvatiyar (2022) also examined the feasibility of an "integrative taxonomy, a systematic review, and research agenda" to develop relevant strategic solutions to address the social difficulties associated with climate change. The implementation and evaluation of Building Resilience Intervention (BRI) were highlighted by Baum, Maharjan, and Langer (2021) in their article on building resilience following the disastrous earthquake in Nepal in 2015; the BRI emphasized the importance of including mental health programs as a part of resilience planning.

Burnett (2023) advised at the 2023 United Nations Climate Change Conference, also known as the 28th Conference of the Parties (COP28), that two common priorities emerged for countries to endeavor to meet the following goals of the Paris Climate Change Agreement ahead of COP28: (i) to respond to the global uptake regarding a global undertaking to seriously address efforts for mitigation, adaptation, and resiliency to address climate change; (ii) to focus on the 'Loss And Damage Fund' which is a reparation package for more prosperous nations, which emit 99% of GHG, to pay to poorer vulnerable countries, such as SIDS, which emit less than 1% of GHG for the damage which GHG has caused to the sustainable development of poorer countries.

According to Worth (2023), "COP28 Agreement Signals 'Beginning of the End' of the Fossil Fuel Era." In their article entitled 'A Less Disastrous Disaster,' Tompkins, Lemos, and Boyd (2008) explored the correlation between efforts to reduce disaster and the long-term adaptive capacity building in the Cayman Islands and NE Brazil. While the two case studies are distinctly different, the need for the successful integration of climate change resiliency planning is essential for the businesses and good governance of both countries and geostrategic factors relating to global warming.

Respitawulan and Rahayu (2019) discussed the role of renewable energy in reducing climate change, which supports the need for resiliency planning in businesses in Indonesia and globally, and, as in the case of the Cayman Islands, to encourage the successful integration of climate change resiliency planning into their businesses. The authors further highlighted the damage to the Indonesian economy from the use of fossil fuel energy. They recommended that their energy diversification policies pursue the development of renewable energy to reduce GHG emissions.

Despite the plethora of scientific literature, including the UN efforts in support of the sagacity of transitioning from fossil fuel energy to renewable energy, there remains strong opposition by specific significant emitters of GHG to fully commit to replacing fossil fuel energy with renewable energy. It is perhaps in this context that Taylor (2014) raised the question: "Can Green Power Save Us from Climate Change?"

Taylor argued that "international efforts to lower carbon emissions have largely failed despite the best intent of Kyoto countries." Taylor substantiated his position by stating that despite the desirable goals of the Kyoto Protocol, which required countries to reduce emissions, the two largest emitters of GHG – China and the United States of America – remain the biggest emitters of GHG.

In Lennon's (2022) commentary on the history of climate change, he stated that it is difficult to forecast the future of "something as complex as global warming"; this position notwithstanding, he predicted that the use of fossil fuels would continue to exacerbate the proliferation of global warming. Lennon further stated that the "United Nations' IPCC tells us that, in order to avoid a global catastrophe, we must reduce emissions by 50% by 2030 and eliminate them by 2050," thus highlighting the critical importance for vulnerable SIDS, such as the Cayman Islands, to seriously consider the integration of climate change resiliency planning into their businesses.

2.3 Climate Change and Its Impact on Businesses

Why is climate change so significant to SIDS, such as the Cayman Islands? According to Hunter (2005), Executive Secretary, UNFCCC, "the answer to this question is simple: these small nations are among the most vulnerable to climate change impacts, which will become critical if no appropriate action is taken." Hunter further stated that "SIDS are among the Parties least responsible for climate change and are dependent on others to ensure that significant action is taken in support of the Convention." In effect, "they strive not only to support the process directly but also to ensure that proper international action is taken to limit emissions of greenhouse gases and to adapt to climate change" (Hunter, 2005).

In their article relating to resilience, Sutcliffe and Vogus (2003) stated that resilience is concerned with maintaining adjustment under challenging conditions. The authors also posited that resilience is not only concerned with a quick return to a normal condition but also involves "learning and growing from the experience, leading to a stronger, more adaptable organization. Mycoo (2017) warned that climate change is a significant challenge for SIDS, such as the Cayman Islands, which makes SIDS particularly vulnerable to economic and environmental losses should the 1.5°C (34.7°F) temperature warming threshold exceed preindustrial (1850-1900) temperatures which was about 13.7°C (56.7°F), which policy was adopted at the 2015 UN Climate Change Conference (COP21) Paris Agreement. Mycoo also expressed concerns that "if globally countries are unable to meet the target of keeping temperatures below 1.5 °C threshold, the vulnerability of Caribbean SIDS will be exacerbated, and impacts are likely to be even more acute."

Limiting warming to 1.5°C would slow the rate of sea level rise, reducing the risk of flooding for millions of people living in coastal areas, such as the Cayman Islands. In support of the dangers of global warming, Scientists at NASA's Goddard Institute for Space Studies have confirmed that "July 2023 was hotter than any other month in the global temperature record" (Bardan, 2004).

2.4 Business Resilience and Climate Change Adaptation

The adaptation of effective strategies is vital to develop climate change resiliency and achieve sustainable development goals (Johnston and Cooper, 2022). Such strategies would include: (i) Implementing policies designed to manage and adapt to the impacts of climate change, such as increased frequency of extreme weather conditions (Berrang-Ford, Ford and Pearson, 2011); (ii) Investment be made in infrastructure which is designed to withstand the impacts of climate change, including water-efficient facilities, and resilient energy systems such as privately owned generators (Hallegatte, Rentschler and Rozenberg, 2019); (iii) Recommendation to restore natural resilience to climate impacts, such as coastal mangrove wetlands that can absorb storm surges (Munang *et al.,* 2013).

Johnston and Cooper (2022) asserted that "Article 7.1 of the Paris Agreement defines a global adaptation goal of enhancing adaptive capacity, strengthening resilience, and reducing vulnerability to climate change." According to Tompkins (2005), initial climate change adaptation in the Cayman Islands between 1988 and 2002 included amendments to the Building Code in 1995/6 and improvements in 2002 to the Government Development and Planning Regulations to increase coastal setbacks of buildings within the Hotel/Tourism zones due to Seven Mile beach erosions (see Appendix 1). Notwithstanding the importance of the foregoing, according to Robinson (2015), SIDS "are among the countries in the world that are most vulnerable to climate change and required to adapt to its impacts; there is little information in the academic literature about how SIDS are adapting to climate change."

2.5 Climate Change in the Cayman Islands

The updated Cayman Islands National Energy Policy (NEP) (2023-2050) focuses on solar renewable energy and the inclusion of new energy resilience policies, such as electric vehicles (EVs), to support the reduction of GHG emissions. The NEP targets: (i) 100% renewable energy by 2050 and (ii) 100% EVs by 2050 (Ministry of Sustainability & Climate Resiliency, 2023). In 2021, the Cayman Islands Government, in partnership with the UK Centre for Ecology and Hydrology, identified the need for the Cayman Islands to increase its climate resiliency, as climate change portends an existential threat to the Cayman Islands, with two of the three Cayman Islands having low-lying topographies (Johnston and Cooper, 2022).

As highlighted in the CCRA report, the top-scoring climate change risks to the Cayman Islands resulted from the devastating impacts of Hurricane Ivan in 2004, which severely damaged coral reefs and caused disruptions to the ecosystem, particularly to the "turtle distribution and population dynamics." According to the CCRA report, of the 50 climate change risks analyzed, 18 were identified as most severe, which include "damage and inundation to the sewerage system and release of wastewater," disruption to the importation of "fossil fuel, power generation, and distribution," and "impacts to communication infrastructure" (Cayman Islands Government, 2022).

According to Weir and Kumar (2020), the integration of renewable energy, as opposed to fossil fuel energy, can make a "country economy more resilient to variations in market prices and fuel imports, by identifying strategies that enhance resilience to accelerating climate change impacts while concurrently reducing GHG." Tompkins, Lemos, and Boyd (2008) stated that "the lesson from the Cayman Islands study is that integrated, learning-based management systems, with wide-spread buy-in and support, can deliver long term risk reduction benefits." Tompkins (2005) stated that initial responses to climate change in the Cayman Islands between 1988 and 2002 included amendments to the Building Code to improve structural integrity and resilience.

Climate change resilience will also consider the following infrastructure and physical adaptations: (i) Upgrading of infrastructure to guard against extreme weather conditions, such as reinforcing buildings against hurricanes and flooding; (ii) Implementation of energy-efficient facilities and the reduction of GHG; (iii) Ensure that adequate water supply is available during droughts; and (iv) Establish adequate emergency plans for business continuity to aid in the quick recovery of businesses after extreme weather events, including adequate insurance coverage. Climate change risks must be regularly monitored to ensure that resiliency plans are functioning effectively. Businesses in the Cayman Islands should ensure that environmental and socio-economic risks are integrated into climate change resiliency strategic planning, which should include adaptations for current impacts, as well as preparation for future force majeure occurrences.

2.6 Factors Influencing the Integration of Climate Change Resiliency

In the discussion on the importance of business resilience, Sidenko (2023) posited that it is essential for both individuals and businesses to be resilient. The author further stated that resiliency is the ability to overcome challenges that present themselves and to recover in a much stronger position successfully. As regards the resiliency of businesses, Sidenko submitted that in addition to anticipating risks and planning for positive outcomes, it is also important to "adapt quickly, prioritize agile methods, learn from failures, and innovate." Equally important is empowering employees' buy-in to the organization's business resiliency plan by developing a resilient culture and promoting trust and effective communication among all stakeholders. Sidenko further stated that resilient leaders must demonstrate the ability to cope with disruptive challenges through appropriate adaptation in the workplace. The enabling factors and barriers that influence the integration of climate change resiliency can be primarily categorized as follows:

2.6.1 Enabling Factors:

- The strength of leadership and good governance of a business operation is essential in determining the successful integration of climate change resiliency, which is positively influenced by the cooperation of the private and public sectors (Berkhout, Hertin, and Gann, 2006).

- Knowledge and awareness of factors relating to climate change impacts and the need to apply remedial adaptation measures are crucial in order to have a considerable effect on the integration of climate change resiliency; appropriate education and training can also enhance the necessary skills (Ekstrom and Moser, 2012).

- The availability and access to adequate financial resources are vital for the implementation and adaptation of resilient measures; this will include funding for research, development of new technologies, and professional application of adaptation activity (Bahinipati, 2011).

- Available regulatory and policy frameworks that encourage or mandate climate change adaptation can prove essential to influence the integration of climate change resiliency, including incentives for "green technologies, building codes, and Government environmental regulations" (Phuong, Biesbroek, and Wals, 2017).

- Utilizing innovative technologies such as AI can improve decision-making and operational efficiency. The resilience of business infrastructure can also improve economic growth and societal well-being "to achieve the United Nations Sustainable Development Goals" (Argyroudis *et al.,* 2021).

2.6.2 Barriers:

- Economic and financial constraints can be barriers to the integration of climate change resiliency; such constraints can create difficulties for small and medium-sized enterprises and developing countries. For example, high costs of importing goods and services create significant challenges for SIDS, such as the Cayman Islands (Mendelsohn, 2012).

24

- Uncertainty related to climate change predictions and the lack of knowledge regarding perceived risks associated with climate change can hinder appropriate decision-making of climate change integration (Jones and Boyd, 2011).

- Inadequate structural and policy frameworks can hamper effective mitigation and climate change adaptation. Societal and cultural factors that may cause community reluctance to change can also negatively influence the integration of climate change resiliency (Adger *et al.,* 2009).

2.7 Effect of Artificial Intelligence (AI) on Climate Change Resiliency

AI is a significant factor that can influence the integration of climate change resiliency by providing better Climate Governance (Bhatia, 2017). According to Bhatia, new and improved innovation tools such as AI will be necessary to cope with the increasing need to mitigate and adapt to the increase and intensity of climate change, thus highlighting the importance for governments and the private sector to integrate AI into their climate change policies. The author has, however, warned that "care has to be taken to ensure that the access to AI and the benefits thereof are equitably distributed to prevent aggravation of inequalities across regions and across nations."

In the context of integrating AI into business resilience systems, Zohuri, Moghaddam, and Mossavar-Rahmani (2022) stressed the importance of improving business resilience with AI, enhanced by machine learning algorithms, which can analyze major data resources and allow businesses to make informed decisions on the negative impacts of climate change. The authors concluded by stating that "Artificial Intelligence is the core for applications and enterprises which use human intelligence for basic functionality" and that "Artificial Intelligence enables us to put our data in a perspective that will work for us rather than overwhelming us with its sheer volume." As climate change increasingly worsens, governments, communities, and businesses will need to take the necessary steps to guard against its negative impacts.

According to Jain *et al.* (2023), to mitigate and adapt to climate change impacts, it will be necessary to utilize practical tools such as AI to adjust to future force majeure occurrences, such as hurricanes, sea level rise, floods, and other extreme weather conditions. By employing the capabilities of AI for adapting to climate change, businesses in the Cayman Islands and globally can seek to improve their resilience and thus develop a sustainable and equitable future for all. However, the use of AI is accompanied by essential compliance requirements of the General Data Protection Regulations (GDPR) relative to privacy and the ethical concerns associated with AI.

2.8 Gaps in the Literature

While there is a large body of research available on climate change resilience, there is limited research that focuses on specific challenges relating to SIDS, such as the Cayman Islands. For example, over the past ten years, four open-source international indices have been developed as measurement tools to examine risks caused by climate change. Unfortunately, no index is explicitly designed for the Caribbean, despite warnings that "countries in the Caribbean region share a common vulnerability and risk of disappearing if the dangers of climate change and global warming are not addressed collectively and urgently" (Grant *et al.,* 2023). Specifically, there is a gap in the literature on how different business sectors, including tourism, financial services, and real estate, can integrate climate change resiliency into businesses in the Cayman Islands.

To explore the perceived gap in the general strategic integration of resilience planning into businesses in the Cayman Islands, the 2023-2040 CICCP aims to deliver a robust strategy to tackle the adverse risks of climate change on the economy, with the view to achieving a Low Carbon-Resilient Economy (Ministry of Sustainability & Climate Resiliency, 2023).

There are limited opportunities for Caribbean countries to implement, monitor, and evaluate progress in the achievement of national and internationally agreed sustainable development goals (SDGs); statistical gaps limit Caribbean countries' ability to develop indicators to measure long-term strides in achieving the SDGs (Camarinhas, 2020).

According to Hunter (2005), Executive Secretary of UNFCCC, "SIDS have not only focused their attention on negotiations of the UNFCCC and its Kyoto Protocol over the past 10 years but also taken a lead in implementing the Convention." Despite this success, SIDS, including the Cayman Islands, are at a disadvantage in making an appreciable reduction in GHG; the impenetrable gap is a result of the large emitters such as China, India, the United States of America and nations within the European Union which emit approximately 99% of GHG as compared to SIDS which emit less than 1% of global emissions (UNDP, 2023).

While there may be some focus on immediate or short-term adaptation measures, other than the Cayman Islands 2023-2050 National Energy Policy and the Cayman Islands 2023-2040 Climate Change Policy, which are still in their embryonic development stages, there are no successful examples of published long-term empirical examples of climate change resiliency integration into businesses in the Cayman Islands.

Chapter 3: Methodology

3.1 Introduction to the Methodology

The Methodology section of this study examined the process by which the research was carried out. Saunder's 'Research Onion' was used as a conceptual framework designed to guide the researcher through the process of developing the research methodology, which consisted of the following six layers: 1) Research Philosophy and Strategy; 2) Research Design; 3) Sample; 4) Ethics; 5) Data Analysis; and 6) Reliability and Validity (Saunders, Lewis, and Thornhill, 2019) (see Appendix 2). This aspect of the dissertation is critical as it not only justified the research approach but also evaluated the appropriateness of the methods, reliability, and validity of the findings.

3.2 Research Methods

There are three main types of research methods: (i) Quantitative research, (ii) Qualitative research, and (iii) Mixed methods research (Saunders, Lewis and Thornhill, 2023). Baxter and Jack (2008) provided qualitative methodology guidance on case study design and implementation to assist research students, which information was supported by Rashid, Rashid and Warraich (2019). Qualitative research methodology was used in this study. In addition to secondary data, primary data was collected through interviews with 10 participants.

3.3 Research Design

Research design represented the second layer of the research and described the overall framework of the case study

29

of the following three critical research methods: (i) Quantitative research, (ii) Qualitative research, and (iii) Mixed methods research. The qualitative research design was selected for this case study, through which primary data was collected, analyzed, and interpreted. On the question of qualitative research design, Hoover (2021) confirmed that there are five standard research designs as follows: (i) *Historical Study*, (ii) *Phenomenology*, (iii) *Grounded Theory*, (iv) *Ethnography*, and (v) *Case Study*, of which the following two theories were used in this research:

Grounded Theory was primarily used to generate new theories and depended solely on the data gleaned through the qualitative research process, which participants in the interview helped to determine. At the same time, the *Case Study* provided an in-depth understanding of the research, which was used to examine information obtained from participants/businesses involved in the in-person interviews. Both the *grounded theory and case study* were essential in the exploratory research and in conducting the in-person interviews. Qualitative research design interviews asked open-ended questions, such as *what, how, why, and explain,* to allow participants the opportunity to give a free-form text answer to elicit discussion, rather than closed-ended questions, such as *was, is, does, and did,* which restricts participants to one of a limited set of possible answers.

3.4 Rationale and Significance

SIDS, such as the Cayman Islands, are highly vulnerable to the negative impacts of climate change, including sea level rise, hurricanes, flooding, and other extreme weather conditions. The analytical evaluation of factors for the successful integration of climate change resiliency planning into businesses in the Cayman Islands is, therefore, of critical importance.

3.5 Research Philosophy and Strategy

The first or outermost layer of the conceptual research onion, which guides the research approach, covers both the research philosophy and strategy layers. In this context, the research philosophy and strategy were based on an epistemological point of view (the theory of knowledge and human life). The researcher supports the view that the three main research philosophies are (i) *Positivism*, (ii) *Interpretivism*, and (iii) *Pragmatism*. *Positivism* asserts that knowledge can only be acquired through factual research, which can be accurately assessed; *Interpretivism* emphasizes the influence that social and cultural factors have on people's thoughts and ideas, while *Pragmatism* examines the research from a commonsense perspective.

The researcher shares the opinion expressed by Phair and Warren (2021) that the actual application of the thought process is more important than the theoretical philosophy relative to an experiment. The research strategy is coordinated with the aim and objectives of the qualitative research design. It includes (i) *Action Research*, (ii) *Case Study Research*, (iii) *Grounded Theory*, and (iv) *Ethnography* (Phair and Warren, 2021).

Action Research helped to inform participants and businesses of problems or weaknesses, with a strong focus on producing actionable as opposed to theoretical input. *Case Study Research* strategy was detailed and provided an in-depth case study for the qualitative research, which is typically inductive in nature; *Grounded Theory,* which is qualitative in nature, provided useful information for the development of the research study; *Ethnography* is a qualitative method, which was used for collecting data from the observation of participants in their natural and cultural environments (Phair and Warren, 2021). Based on a pragmatic view of the foregoing analogous process relating to the 'research onion,' the researcher utilized an inductive qualitative approach to peel back the six layers of the research study.

3.6 Qualitative Case Study Research

As regards the qualitative case study research, Baxter and Jack (2008) posited that "the qualitative case study is an approach that facilitates exploration of a phenomenon within its context using a variety of data sources." In this case study research, primary data were collected through in-person interviews with 10 participants, and secondary data were collected through the literature review. The qualitative inductive research provided observations from the in-person interviews with the participants, which produced themes upon which theories were established, instead of quantitative deductive research, which begins with a theory upon which the hypothesis is tested (Snieder and Larner, 2009).

In their discussion on qualitative case study research, Bryman and Bell (2011) posited that inductive research allows the researcher to develop a new theory instead of using an existing theory available in quantitative deductive research. This qualitative case study research also considered the emphasis of Saunders and Tosey (2013) relating to the importance and in-depth choices available in qualitative case study research.

The qualitative case study research was specifically chosen due to the comprehensive and in-depth nature of the interview questions required to elicit appropriate information relating to the integration of climate change resiliency planning into businesses in the Cayman Islands. This case study was compelling in capturing variables relating to the following research question: "What perceived factors can successfully integrate climate change resiliency planning into businesses in the Cayman Islands?" This question was answered through the collection and analysis of primary and secondary research data. Also, the specific themes that emerged throughout the in-person participant interviews prioritized the need for businesses to strengthen the structural integrity of their buildings and other business facilities to guard against the intensity of hurricane-force winds and increasing sea level rise, which presages future catastrophic destruction due to the negative impacts of climate change, primarily due to the low topography of the Cayman Islands.

3.7 Sample

The third layer of the research highlighted the sample size consisting of 10 participants, selected through the purposive and convenience sampling method, based on the small target population who could be available for in-person interviews and the experience and capability of the participants to provide in-depth data. Research interviews generally use a purposive sampling approach to select participants; purposive sampling comprises participants based on the characteristics of a population and the objectives of the research. The process used for the recruitment of the 10 participants was by phone calls and emails, which enabled the researcher to contact stakeholders, professional groups, or others with knowledge or expertise of the research questions. Potential participants included owners of businesses, chief executive officers, presidents, directors, partners, and other senior officers. The business entities consisted of a cross-section of small to large organizations engaged in a variety of services in the Cayman Islands. These criteria enabled the researcher to select 10 participants based on the characteristics required in the purposive sample and who were capable of engaging in an intelligent discussion on each of the five interview questions, which were consistent with the research objectives.

It was against this background that a qualitative cross-sectional research was conducted, which included Government and private sector participants who were carefully selected to ensure that the sample size included a fair demographic representation of participants within the various businesses in the Cayman Islands; the sample also enabled the capture of the different themes, where possible establish thematic analysis for analyzing the qualitative data and evaluate and explore perspectives of participants directly involved and/or well informed about climate change resiliency planning in the Cayman Islands.

3.8 Development of Interview Questions

The following Table highlights the consistency of the aim and objectives of the research as outlined in Chapter 1.2. Details of the interview questions are attached (see Appendix

3). The interview questions were aligned with the research objectives, as discussed in the following Table:

3.8.1 Table: Research Objectives and Interview Questions

Research Objectives	Interview Questions
To explore current international trends for resiliency planning and determine an evaluation of resilience in businesses in the Cayman Islands.	Given your experience of the catastrophic damage caused by Hurricane Ivan and/or by the COVID-19 pandemic, what measures have been taken to strengthen the resiliency of your business?
To gather a range of perspectives from key stakeholders in the Cayman Islands and identify any perceived barriers to obtaining CICCP's vision relating to the integration of climate change resilience into business strategies.	What are your perspectives regarding the ability of the Cayman Islands Climate Change Policy (2023-2040) to promote and sustain the integration of climate change resilience into business strategies over these 17 years?
To analyze underlying factors for, or barriers against, successful implementation of resiliency programs by critically assessing the impact of local and international policies relating to resiliency in	What specific resilience and adaptation measures has your business implemented to cope with extreme climate change challenges such as the rise in sea levels, flooding, and hurricane-force winds?

businesses in the Cayman Islands.	
To assess the current state of climate resiliency planning currently integrated into business practices in the Cayman Islands to determine any existing gaps and strengths.	What innovative practices or technologies has your business adopted to enhance climate change resiliency and sustainability?
To derive conclusions and, based on the analysis, propose actionable recommendations for the future practice of business in the Cayman Islands to integrate resiliency into their operations successfully.	Does your business prioritize and allocate protective measures, such as insurance coverage, to integrate resiliency into your business operations successfully? Also, in view of the importance of buy-in by management and staff, has your business experienced resistance to the implementation of climate change resiliency measures? If so, please explain.

3.9 Research Ethics

The fourth layer of this research considered: (i) the Informed Consent Form for participation in research relating to the integration of climate change resiliency into businesses in the Cayman Islands was read and signed by each of the participants at the beginning of each in-person interview and by the researcher. The Informed Consent Form also provided the participant's right to withdraw at any time. The researcher ensured that each participant understood the terms of the Informed Consent Form before commencing with the interview (see Appendix 4) and (ii) the anonymity of each participant is protected by the use of alphabetical codes (A-J). Confidentiality is guaranteed in compliance with the GDPR. The GDPR is a European Union (EU) law that came into effect on 25th May 2018, which governs the way in which we can use, process, and store personal data (information about an identifiable living person).

3.9.1 Data Analysis

The fifth layer of the research discussed how the data analysis was processed and analyzed to draw conclusions, which involved qualitative analysis methods such as thematic analysis and highlighted specific themes relating directly to the research aim and objectives. Member checking was also used to validate the accuracy of the interpretation of the interviews. The researcher complied with the following view expressed by Braun and Clarke (2021): "Researchers must choose between a diverse range of approaches that can differ considerably in their underlying (but often implicit) conceptualizations of qualitative research, meaningful knowledge production, and key constructs such as themes, as well as analytic procedures." In this connection, the researcher conducted a thematic analysis to establish the consistency of any themes observed that were considered relevant to the research question.

3.9.2 Reliability and Validity

The sixth layer of the research examined the reliability and validity concepts to evaluate the quality of the study. The process highlighted the veracity and authenticity of the method and techniques used to analyze the primary data. Reliability was basically focused on the consistency of the analytical testing, while validity was concerned with the accuracy and integrity of the findings. Both reliability and validity played an essential role in determining the rigorous standards to which qualitative research was subjected to ensure the integrity of the research findings. Further details are provided hereunder on these two essential research concepts:

3.9.3 Reliability

Reliability was concerned with the dependability and consistency of the research methods over time. According to Golafshani (2003), "To ensure reliability in qualitative research, examination of trustworthiness is crucial." Dependability and consistency underpinned the trustworthiness of the reliability of this research. The researcher demonstrated research dependability and consistency by maintaining thorough records of the research activities to ensure that the process was transparent and could be critically evaluated by others.

3.9.4 Validity

Validity was broadly focused on the accuracy and truthfulness of the findings. Several specific types of validity were considered, including Credibility (Guba & Lincoln, 1994), Confirmability (Morrow, 2005), and Authenticity (Guba & Lincoln, 1989). Credibility involved establishing that the results were accurate from the perspective of the participants in the research; the techniques used to enhance credibility included observation and member checking (where participants reviewed and confirmed the findings). Confirmability considered the extent to which the results were corroborated through repeated reviews of the findings, and diverse and independent observations and viewpoints among the participants achieved Authenticity.

Chapter 4: Results of Primary Data

4.1 Introduction to the Results of Primary Data Collection

The aims and objectives of collecting primary data are crucial to the research process, as they guide the direction and purpose of the research study. The primary aims were to generate firsthand data, ensure the originality of the data collected, and ascertain the relevance and consistency of the research questions relative to the research objectives. Further, the primary data provided empirical evidence in support of the decision-making process, and in particular, the strategic and policy development relative to the successful integration of climate change resiliency planning into businesses in the Cayman Islands. The objectives supported the aims of the research study by identifying and analyzing themes within the primary data collected from the in-person interviews of the 10 participants, anonymously classified as Codes A-J to protect their confidentiality. By setting clear aims and objectives, the researcher was able to ensure the viability and validity of the overall success and integrity of the research.

4.2 Data Collection

The procedure for data collection from interview participants involved several key steps to ensure that the process was orderly, systematic, ethical, and practical, which included: (i) a clear explanation of the purpose and objectives of the interview to guide the data collection process; (ii) the development of a structured interview with open-ended questions relevant to the research objectives; (iii) all questions were clear, unbiased and organized to elicit detailed responses; (iv) a purposive sampling strategy was used to select participants who were capable of providing relevant contributions to the various interview questions.

Upon confirmation from the potential participants of their willingness to participate, a mutually convenient schedule was agreed upon for in-person interviews. At the beginning of each interview, the researcher explained to the participant that the questions would be read by the researcher and responses typed; at the end of each interview, the participant was given the opportunity to review their responses and make any necessary amendments. Each interview was conducted in an office setting and lasted for an average duration of one hour.

4.3 Findings

4.3.1 Participant Profiles

Alphabetical Coding (A-J) was used to protect the identities of each of the 10 participants. Within SIDs such as the Cayman Islands, where many individuals and businesses are well known to each other, every effort has been made to protect the identities of the participants fully. The following are brief profiles of participants using their alphabetical codes.

- **CODE A:** This participant is the owner and CEO of a small computer company, which offers a wide range of services in the business of information technology, including sales and servicing of desktop and laptop computers, peripheral devices such as keyboards, printers, networking equipment, routers, modems, and supporting software such as Microsoft Office. The participant advised that technologies are now becoming standard, such as working remotely through the use of technology; post-COVID-19 pandemic, working remotely is becoming everyday use and not just during disasters. Also, business certifications and education must be current, and the majority of the education is from global companies such as Microsoft and Google. The participant stated that their customers also adapt their services to meet challenges and to provide solutions to remedy or mitigate the problems that may occur.

On the question of protective measures, such as insurance coverage, to successfully integrate resiliency into business operations, the participant stated that, in view of the cost constraints relating to insurance coverage, it is not financially feasible for small businesses like his to undertake the high cost of insurance coverage.

- **CODE B:** This participant is the owner and president of a large construction company providing design, development, construction, and property services and is one of the Cayman Islands' leading residential, commercial, and hospitality developers and service providers. As an award-winning property developer, the company has adopted the following motto: 'Pursuit of Excellence.' This standard is maintained by its well-trained employees, including its in-house architects, quantity surveyors, geothermal experts, and risk assessors. As regards adaptation and resilience measures, its policy is to build 7-8 feet above sea level to protect against flooding and sea level rise. The company has also exceeded the legal setback requirement by the Planning Department of Government relating to the construction of buildings on the shoreline. It is compliant with the Cayman Islands' Building Code, which is based on the South Florida Building Code.

- **CODE C:** This participant represents an organization that is part of a large global entity and has developed policies and procedures that assist in mitigating catastrophic risks to its business, staff, customers, and infrastructure. The policies and processes undergo testing and adaptation on an annual basis in and across various markets where it operates. The organization is partially dependent on the physical external plant infrastructure of some other utility companies for part of the service delivery. This dependency has, however, been on the decline over the decades as new technologies have been introduced to place more infrastructure support below ground. The company's infrastructure has for a number of years been located undersea – the company having moved from satellite dish-based redundancy. As regards direct connections to the customers, the company has transitioned to underground cables that are more resistant to the negative impacts of climate change.

- **CODE D:** This participant is the director of an organization that is focused on mitigation issues relative to force majeure occurrences, including hurricanes and earthquakes. To prevent damage and improve structural safety, preparedness, and planning are key to ensuring an effective outcome from the perspectives of individuals and the community. A primary objective of this organization is to enhance the resiliency of the Cayman Islands against the negative impacts of climate change. In this connection, this organization is implementing and rolling out a flood sensor pilot program, and it is hoped that similar programs will be installed across the three Cayman Islands, providing improved forecasting and understanding of flood threats, as well as providing the basis for public awareness and outreach programs related to flood threats. This organization has available shelter capacity for the general public. Storm Surge and Wave Impact Modelling studies are also in progress.

- **CODE E:** This participant is the owner of a company that focuses its attention on operational resiliency, which allows it to withstand, adapt, and recover from disruptive events; it is housed in a category 5 rated hurricane warehouse shelter which is elevated 10 feet above sea level, with a mezzanine located at 25 feet above sea level. The company is equipped with solar and battery power as stand-by power, enabling it to work remotely up to the time of the installation of its renewable energy projects. In view of the nature of the business, which involves solar renewables installation and servicing, much time is spent on compliance with Government policies and regulations. The company also provides its customers with advice on appropriate mitigation, adaptation, and resiliency measures.

- **CODE F:** This participant is a vice president of an organization that provides essential services to the general public. In the late 90s, the organization upgraded the structural integrity and general hardening of its buildings to protect itself against category 5 hurricanes. Their mitigation, adaptation, and resiliency measures include appropriate standards for wind resistance for all of their buildings, flood plain levels, and the installation of critical infrastructure facilities underground. The organization has extensive preparedness plans for various disasters, including hurricanes and fires, stand-by supplies, and agreements with key overseas suppliers to ensure easy access within the supply chain. Since Hurricane Ivan, the organization has installed 3 new indoor facilities together with several other resiliency improvements to the company's infrastructure.

- **CODE G:** This participant is a partner in a firm that provides legal and financial services, and the company's practice is primarily in local legal services. As regards climate change impacts, the office building is compliant with the Cayman Islands' Building Code. The participant explained that the office space leased by the company was constructed to withstand hurricane-force winds but expressed concerns regarding the 8-foot tidal surges experienced during Hurricane Ivan, and he commented that flooding was of more concern to his office than hurricane-force winds. It was further suggested that as a protection against flooding, future buildings should have higher foundations. Regarding the COVID-19 pandemic, as in the case of other participants, the participant advised that the office staff were able to work from home seamlessly and, in some instances, more efficiently and that the company has plans to relocate their servers offshore to protect their communication capabilities, and advised that all of their data and files are electronic.

- **CODE H:** This participant is a senior officer of a company that provides an essential utility service to the general public. As a result of the damage caused to their buildings during Hurricane Ivan, it was necessary to harden the structural integrity of their buildings, which effectively enhanced the structural resilience of their business.

To further protect their operational facilities, they have undertaken a comprehensive approach to enhance the resilience of the company's business activities generally. To strengthen the use of this critical public utility, a new and well-equipped Command Centre was built together with added facilities provided for the staff. This public utility has installed flood gates at every entrance and drain plugs to prevent water ingress during flooding; these additions are critical in maintaining the integrity and functionality of the facilities during adverse conditions. In addition to the flood gates, windows at all of the company's facilities are hurricane rated, or otherwise protected by hurricane shutters; protocols have been developed to safely secure assets prior to the occurrence of extreme weather events, which includes anchoring equipment and protecting vulnerable components to minimize damage and ensure rapid recovery, and relocating and storing critical equipment in predetermined safe areas.

During the COVID-19 pandemic, the participant had customer service staff set up to work from home, as well as equipping their fieldwork crews with personal protection equipment and test kits. The senior officer ensured that the organization was well equipped during the disaster caused by Hurricane Ivan, as well as the difficulties resulting from the COVID-19 pandemic.

- **CODE I:** This participant, who is a senior officer, explained that this public entity tends to think of resiliency issues in terms of preparation to mitigate against winds, flooding, and other physical climate hazards. But the financial resiliency of a business, including the Government with its portfolio of owned and managed assets is also critical. From the financial perspective, this entity is able to examine the reports of the United Nations Economic Commission for Latin America and the Caribbean (UNECLAC), which have been prepared following the major hurricanes in the Cayman Islands, such as Ivan, Paloma, and Gustav. The participant stressed that the Cayman Islands is not recognized as a SIDS at the Climate Conventions because the Cayman Islands are not a sovereign body but rather recognized as an Associate State or UK Overseas Territory, which has proven to be problematic due to the lack of recognition. However, the participant opined that as the Cayman Islands Premier now chairs the meeting of the United Kingdom Overseas Territories Association (UKOTA), the issues regarding non-recognition of the Associated States (including the Cayman Islands) may be dealt with in a timely manner.

This participant further stated that bureaucracy is a limiting factor to moving things forward in a timely manner to achieve targets set out in the updated National

Energy Policy (mirrored in the CICCP). Also, accountability is essential, but micromanagement is an issue that creates challenges in accomplishing goals for energy security and adaptation measures.

- **CODE J:** According to this senior officer, the Cayman Islands Government (CIG), the largest employer in the Islands, has done quite a bit of work since Hurricane Ivan, which was refined after COVID-19 to ensure the resiliency of the CIG and Cayman Islands businesses. One such accomplishment was restructuring the National Hurricane Committee, now renamed Hazard Management Cayman Islands (HMCI). Before COVID, the focus was on hurricane resiliency, but after COVID, the focus was more on resiliency planning.

  The Government is adapting to the Joint Emergency Service Continuity of Business and the Joint Emergency Service Interoperability Programme (JESIP) approach to hazard response. That framework and response are what CIG is working toward, with "a lot of work going into that framework." For example, Methane is one of the dropdowns under JESIP. The participant further stated that the Government has a good building code and that improvements to that code are continuing as it works toward resiliency for private and public entities.

  According to the participant, it wasn't structural damage that was the primary concern post-Ivan, but instead, it was the flooding issues. The Cayman Islands are part of the Caribbean Catastrophe Risk Insurance Facility (CCRIF) and are members of the Caribbean Disaster Emergency

Management Agency (CDEMA). The challenge for the Cayman Islands is that CIG is a large entity with many departments, some of which operate in silos, and there are also perceptions relating to current cost-benefit considerations.

4.3.2 Thematic Analysis

The researcher created a working document to assist in the analysis of the responses to the five interview questions. Under each of the five questions, the responses of each of the 10 participants to the particular question were set out. This design facilitated the analysis by the researcher, enabling the following brief themes to be identified; these are discussed in more detail under Chapter 5.1:

- **Awareness of Climate Change:** This was a key point highlighted in the interviews with each of the 10 participants, whose responses are briefly summarized in Codes A-J of the foregoing section. This analysis is comprised of the verbal nuances of the participants, together with any essential non-verbal cues observed.

- **Planning and Strategies:** There were profound lessons learned from Hurricane Ivan, which was the common theme of the participants relative to the need for planning and strategies. As a result, businesses have implemented operational manuals on how to prepare for the mitigation, adaptation, and resiliency of force majeure events, including hurricanes, pandemics, and other disasters.

- **Challenges and Barriers:** Common challenges and barriers highlighted in this theme included socio-economic issues of small businesses, such as the high cost of insurance coverage for their businesses; the cost of mitigation, adaptation, and resiliency was also challenging. The initial high cost of transitioning to technologies that emit low levels of GHG, such as solar photovoltaics (PV) renewables, was also identified as a potential barrier.

- **Recommendations and Future Directions:** The common theme relating to recommendations and future directions focused on innovations, including the possible utility of AI products and the need to upgrade existing technologies.

Chapter 5: Discussion

5.1 Interpretation of Findings

To interpret the findings in the context of the literature review and the specific context of SIDS, it was important to interpret these findings by comparing them with the existing secondary data, which highlighted the particular characteristics and challenges of SIDS, such as the Cayman Islands. This comparison was based on the research question: "What perceived factors can successfully integrate climate resiliency planning into businesses in the Cayman Islands?"

The evaluation of this question revealed that the literature review aligned with the findings relative to climate change resiliency planning in the Cayman Islands. In this connection, the literature review addressed climate change challenges globally, including SIDS, such as the Cayman Islands, and found that climate change was largely human-induced and that 99% of GHG was caused by large countries such as China, the United States of America, the European Union, India, Russia and Japan, and that less than 1% of GHG was emitted by the 57 SIDS worldwide, including the Cayman Islands (Ortega-Ruiz *et al.,* 2022).

Although the findings suggest the need for strong local government support and that regulatory frameworks are essential for successful climate change resilience, based on the empirical evidence that large countries emit 99% of GHG, it is reasonable to conclude that these large countries are mainly responsible for the negative impacts of global climate change. It is against this background that the COP28 (2023) recommended that vulnerable countries such as SIDS should benefit from the 'Loss and Damage Fund for Developing Countries,' which was established by the UN Climate Change Conference (COP27) in 2022 to create a fund to help low-income developing SIDS specifically offset the damage from the natural disasters caused by climate change (UNDP, 2024).

Questions on the specific vulnerabilities of SIDS, such as the Cayman Islands, were also raised by Tompkins and Hurlston (2005) on natural hazards and climate change and by Tompkins, Hurlston, and Poortinga (2009) on disaster resilience. 'Key Findings' in the thematic analysis revealed the following four distinct themes: (i) Awareness of Climate Change, (ii) Planning and Strategies, (iii) Challenges and Barriers, and (iv) Recommendations and Future Directions. In view of the importance of the thematic analysis briefly discussed in Chapter 4.4.2 of this study, a more detailed expansion of the earlier discussions, supported by the literature review, is provided hereunder:

- **Theme 1: Awareness of Climate Change** was discussed, and participants raised concerns regarding the impacts of climate change and recognized the need to strengthen the resiliency of their businesses. The participants also articulated the importance of hardening the structural integrity of their buildings based on firsthand experience with the catastrophic impact of Hurricane Ivan in 2004. Mycoo (2017) expressed concerns that climate change is a significant problem for SIDS, which makes them particularly vulnerable to economic and environmental losses. On the question as to why climate change is so crucial to SIDS, such as the Cayman Islands, Hunter (2005), Executive Secretary of UNFCC, commented that small nations are among the most vulnerable to climate change.

According to Ekstrom and Moser (2012), knowledge and awareness of factors relating to climate change impacts, mitigation, and the need for adaptation measures are important factors in strengthening climate change resiliency. Further, this awareness was heightened by the predictions from hurricane specialists such as the NOAA's National Hurricane Center (NHC) relating to frequent and increased intensity of future hurricanes. Most participants asserted that their primary concern was sea level rise and flooding, as opposed to hurricane force winds.

- **Theme 2: Planning and Strategies** were based on the lessons learned from Hurricane Ivan, including the adoption of building standards to withstand category 5 hurricanes and increasing the floor height of buildings to protect against events such as sea level rises, storm surges, and flooding. One of the large public utility providers, which experienced severe flooding and storm surges, has hardened the structure of its buildings by installing concrete roofing, in addition to elevating the floor height of new buildings to six feet above the mean sea level. These measures suggested by interview participants align with recommendations by Johnston and Cooper (2022), that adaptation of effective strategies is vital to develop climate change resiliency.

In addition, Berrang-Ford, Ford, and Pearson (2011) posited the importance of implementing policies designed to manage and adapt to the impact of climate change. Some businesses have protected critical infrastructure by installing it underground, as well as increasing the height of floor levels in new buildings to guard against sea level rise and flooding, particularly; others have strengthened their buildings by installing hurricane-resistant windows and doors. The ability to work from home was also viewed as a key component of strategies to ensure business continuity.

These strategies are also comparable to the existing literature by Hallegatte, Rentschler, and Rozenberg (2019), who recommended that investments be made in infrastructure that is designed to withstand the impacts of climate change, including water-efficient facilities and resilient energy systems such as privately owned generators. Munang *et al.* (2013) recommended the restoration of natural resilience to climate impacts, such as coastal mangrove wetlands that can absorb storm surges, which is comparable to the restoration of erosion of coastal areas within the Cayman Islands.

- **Theme 3: Challenges and Barriers** were identified, including socio-economic issues of businesses in the Cayman Islands, such as the high cost of insurance coverage, cost of mitigation, adaptation, and resiliency. The initial cost of transitioning to technologies that emit low levels of GHG, such as solar photovoltaic renewables, was also identified as a potential barrier. To address this challenge, the Government is working on duty concessions to enable the private sector to import energy-efficient machinery and equipment. As regards the high costs of integration of climate change resiliency, Mendelsohn (2012) also recognized that economic and financial constraints could create challenges and barriers for small and medium-sized enterprises and developing countries. As regards EVs, a participant observed that there is a challenge and potential health hazard regarding the risks associated with the disposal of replacement batteries for EVs, as well as disposing of the dangerous gases emitted in discarding high-tech x-ray machines used in medical facilities. As regards the disposal of discarded batteries, one participant advised that their overseas manufacturers have indicated that they would take back batteries used in the participant's company when they need recycling, so this company does not have a problem in that area. As noted from the foregoing, there were mixed challenges and barriers among the participants.

A participant also observed that despite the concessions provided by the Government in lowering the import duties on EVs, Government bureaucracy is a challenge to efficiency, and also commented that while accountability in Government is necessary, micromanagement is an issue that creates challenges in accomplishing the goals required for energy security and adaptation measures. The comparable challenges and barriers in the existing literature are highlighted in the difficulties the United Nations is experiencing in obtaining enforceable commitments at the Conference of the Parties (COP) meetings, as reflected in the non-binding Agreement to transition away from fossil fuels adopted at COP28 in 2023.

- **Theme 4: Recommendations and Future Directions** were discussed, with specific reference to innovations, including the possible utility of AI products and the need to upgrade existing technologies. Also, one participant recommended using geothermal technology as a renewable energy source for cooling buildings, aiming to eventually replace fossil fuels currently used to generate electricity for air conditioning. This technology is already being installed in that participant's building developments. Another participant recommended the use of AI-enabled chatbot support for more efficient responses to customers; this participant also made recommendations for future directions, including underground cables, fiber optic cables, cloud-based storage, data encryption, international organization for standardization (ISO) certification for employees, and knowledge sharing across countries and legal jurisdictions.

In this connection, the literature review provided recommendations and future directions, including the use of AI innovations to assist in the integration of climate change resiliency (Bhatia, 2017). Similarly, Zohuri, Moghaddam, and Mossavar-Rahmani (2022) highlighted the importance of improving business resiliency with AI. As regards the way forward, a participant advised that their organization had adopted several practices and technologies to support climate change resiliency and sustainability across their business operations, including smart technology, which is a feature of several aspects of their business operations; smart technology maximizes performance efficiency, which results in reduced energy costs. By integrating innovative practices and technologies in their operation, this participant aims to not only enhance their resilience to climate change impacts but also contribute to a more sustainable future for the community and the environment.

The use of innovative technologies, such as AI, to improve decision-making operational efficiency was recommended by Argyroudis *et al.* (2021). As regards the implementation of the CICCP, participants were generally of the view that the Government would need to create programs and frameworks for businesses and members of the public to follow, as well as enshrine some of the policies in legislation to ensure that specific goals are met. Phuong, Biesbroek, and Wals (2017) noted that regulatory and policy frameworks that encourage or mandate climate change adaptation could prove essential to influence the integration of climate change resiliency.

5.2 Comparison with Literature

The findings in the primary data, as compared with the secondary data, provided the foundation for the aim of the study, which critically analyzed the perceived barriers to successful integration of resiliency planning into businesses in the Cayman Islands; the research objectives support the aim, and the Interview Questions were developed in alignment with the research objectives (see Table 4.3.1). The use of both primary and secondary data is essential in amalgamating a critical analysis of the dissertation topic, and it strengthens the validity and reliability of the research. Secondary data contributes historical context and background information, while qualitative primary data can add depth and authenticity to the research findings. Integrating secondary and primary data allows the research process to benefit from a broader and higher-quality research outcome. By comparing the findings with the literature and theoretical frameworks, the study emphasizes consistent themes while also contributing new insights specific to the Cayman Islands and SIDS context. This comparison highlights the multifaceted nature of climate resilience planning and the importance of tailored strategies that consider local conditions and challenges.

5.3 Implications for Practice

The implications for businesses in the Cayman Islands and other SIDS relative to climate change resiliency are significant. These small island developing states are particularly vulnerable to the negative impacts of climate change due to their geographic, economic, and low-lying characteristics. In this connection, these businesses must prepare appropriate risk management assessments to identify and address specific vulnerabilities, such as the impacts of sea level rise, flooding, and other disruptions caused by extreme weather events. Financial preparedness, such as emergency funds and access to insurance coverage, is crucial to cope with and recover from climate change impacts; the development and engagement in strong community relationships are critical in addressing various types of force majeure events, such as hurricanes and earthquakes. For businesses in the Cayman Islands and similar

SIDS, addressing implications for practice involves a multifaceted approach that integrates risk management, sustainable practices, financial preparedness, and community engagement. Proactive preparation by SIDS, such as the Cayman Islands, can enhance the resilience of their businesses and ensure long-term viability and sustainability.

5.4 Implications for Policy

Based on the findings from the primary data of 10 interviews regarding the climate change resiliency of businesses in the Cayman Islands, potential policy recommendations could include (i) The implementation and enforcement of codes and infrastructure standards that would address the negative impacts of extreme climate change events such as hurricanes, flooding, sea level rise, and hurricane-force winds; (ii) Encourage the introduction of tax incentives for businesses to invest in renewable energy such as solar energy, and certification of technologies such as geothermal cooling systems to reduce, and eventually replace fossil fuel emitters of GHG; (iii) Strengthen emergency preparedness and response strategies for businesses, by mandating appropriate mitigation, adaptation, and resiliency strategies. In this connection, Government could consider the establishment of financial facilities to assist businesses in obtaining funding assistance to invest in resilience measures, as well as encourage banking and/or other financial institutions to assist businesses with low-interest loans to support businesses in building necessary climate resilience; and (iv) Encourage collaboration between Government and the private sector to develop Private-Public-Partnerships (PPPs) to finance repair, replacement, and introduction of new facilities such as roads, water facilities, schools, and healthcare facilities, which could directly or indirectly positively impact the recovery and sustainability of businesses in the Cayman Islands.

The foregoing potential policy recommendations extracted from the primary data contribute to a holistic approach to improving climate change resiliency in the Cayman Islands.

Chapter 6: Conclusion

6.1 Summary of Key Findings

In summary, the key findings from the primary data provided important qualitative clarity into the research topic, which examined a "critical analysis of perceived factors for successful integration of climate change resiliency planning into businesses in the Cayman Islands"; key themes also emerged from the primary data (see 4.4 Findings). As evident from the responses, the participants understood the interview questions and were able to provide knowledgeable contributions in the interview process. They also articulated various challenges and barriers requiring attention and their plans to address such issues wherever possible effectively. Overall, the key findings from the interviews provided a comprehensive understanding of the research topic.

6.2 Contributions to Knowledge

The research topic contributes to climate change resiliency in several fundamental ways, including: (i) By critically analyzing the perceived factors that contribute to the successful integration of climate change resiliency planning, the research was able to identify the most important issues that businesses need to address; (ii) The primary and secondary data examined the challenges and barriers that businesses face trying to integrate climate change resiliency into their operations, as well as enable and facilitate the business operations; (iii) It is hoped that this research will provide an informative resource for Government, highlight best practices within the business community, and thus help to build overall community resilience.

In effect, this research contributes to knowledge by providing critical insights into the basis for resiliency planning and accordingly supports the development of a more resilient, sustainable, and prosperous business environment capable of withstanding the negative impacts of climate change.

6.3 Limitations

In conducting the research study on the "critical analysis of perceived factors for successful integration of climate change resiliency planning into businesses in the Cayman Islands," there are a number of limitations that could potentially impact the findings and conclusions, including the following:

- A small sample size of the research study could lead to limitations and biases. However, the researcher ensured that this study was strongly supported by a selected sample size of 10 knowledgeable participants. When deciding between selective sampling (also known as purposive sampling) and, say, random sampling, the choice hinged on the population and the specific circumstances of the research study. Also, the study required participants with particular characteristics, knowledge, and experience that are not uniformly distributed across the general population.

- To avoid concerns about confidentiality, the identities of participants were protected by the use of alphabetical Codes A-J, with a Code representing the name of each of the 10 participants, bearing in mind the difficulty but importance of protecting anonymity within a small population, such as the Cayman Islands.

- The researcher remained conscious that the research study relied on perceived factors, which by nature are inherently subjective and thus could vary significantly between the participants. Also, despite the diverse cross-section of participants interviewed, the researcher did not detect any evidence of bias, misinterpretation of questions, or gaps that could affect the accuracy and reliability of the data collected. While appreciating the possible limitations that may arise in research studies, the researcher is satisfied with the robustness and veracity of this research study.

6.4 Recommendations for Research on Visible and Hidden Costs of Climate Change

6.4.1 Visible Costs

Recommendations for future research could include (i) Longitudinal research to ascertain changes in perceptions, practices, and outcomes over time and to determine how businesses adapt to climate change; (ii) Comparative studies of the Cayman Islands with other SIDS could provide information on common challenges and share knowledge of successful strategies to inform best practices; (iii) Consideration could be given to use both qualitative and quantitative research-methods to provide more in-depth research conclusions. For example, while qualitative methodology provides deep insights into perceptions and experiences, quantitative methodology has the added capability of providing statistical validation and empirical evidence in support of research conclusions; (iv) Economic and financial analyses can be conducted to determine the cost-benefit of implementing specific climate change resiliency measures; and (v) Future research studies can build upon current research, and address any limitations raised in previous research studies, and expand the scope of more comprehensive knowledge of climate change resiliency planning into businesses in the Cayman Islands.

As regards recommendations for future research, it is of interest to factor into future research the damaging potentials of extreme weather conditions on the overall economy of the Cayman Islands. The three main economic sectors or three legs of the economy are (i) Financial Services, (ii) Tourism, and (iii) Real Estate and Construction. The experiences of the catastrophic impacts of Hurricane Ivan on 11-12 September 2004 (see Appendix 5), on which several books were written, including a comprehensive recording entitled 'Paradise Interrupted' (Lawrence and Platt, 2005), vividly portrayed the appalling devastation wreaked on Grand Cayman by Hurricane Ivan. The following is an extract from the introduction in the book 'Paradise Interrupted' by the Governor, Mr. Bruce H. Dinwiddy, CMG: "This book carries a message of hope, but also a warning. Ivan will not be the last hurricane to strike our Islands. We all pray that nothing like it will follow for a long time. But we were blessed last September that the peak of the storm came by day and that the highest sea surge coincided with low tide. We must all digest and remember the lessons from Ivan and remain vigilant to ensure we are even more successful in riding out the next huge storm to cross our corner of the Caribbean, whenever that may be."

From an economic perspective, extreme weather events, such as Hurricane Ivan, can cause extensive damage to hotels, resorts, airports, roads, and other critical infrastructure, particularly essential for tourism. The degradation of natural attractions can, for example, reduce the Islands' appeal as a tourist destination, which can lead to devastating economic impacts on the Cayman Islands. As in the case of the financial services and the real estate and construction sectors of the Cayman Islands' 'three-legged economy,' tourism is a significant source of employment and income for local communities that sustain businesses in the Cayman Islands. A decline in tourist arrivals due to extreme weather can lead to job losses and reduced income for those dependent on tourism, thus exacerbating economic vulnerability. Many local businesses, including restaurants, shops, and tour operators, rely on tourism, and reduced tourist spending can negatively impact these businesses, leading to closures and economic downturns in the community. Equally important is the reputational damage that extreme weather can foist upon the Cayman Islands as a safe and desirable tourist destination; extreme climate change poses significant threats to the tourism sector in the Cayman Islands, affecting infrastructure, operational costs, tourist activities, safety, local economies, and the destination's reputation.

Addressing these challenges and barriers requires a comprehensive approach that includes investing in resilient infrastructure, implementing effective disaster preparedness and response strategies, and promoting sustainable tourism practices and improved port facilities.

In summary, the three economic legs – financial services, tourism, real estate, and construction- form the foundation of the Cayman Islands' economy, each contributing significantly to the overall economic growth of the territory. The interaction between these sectors supports a diversified economic base, although each one also faces challenges related to global financial conditions, regulatory changes, and environmental impacts.

In addition to discussions in Chapter 2.7 on AI, future research directions may also consider the advantages and disadvantages of following enhanced efficiency and productivity by using innovative technologies such as AI. Integrating AI into businesses in SIDS, such as the Cayman Islands, presents several advantages and disadvantages, including the following:

- **Advantages:**

i.   AI can automate routine and repetitive tasks, freeing up human resources for more strategic and creative work, thus resulting in reduced costs and higher productivity.

ii. AI is capable of analyzing large amounts of data quickly, allowing businesses to make more informed decisions and effectively improve operational procedures.

iii. AI can be used to tailor services to customer preferences, leading to increased sales and customer retention.

iv. AI can enhance data management and datasets more efficiently (Argyroudis *et al.*, 2021).

- **Disadvantages:**

i. The implementation of AI technologies requires significant initial expenditure, including training, infrastructure, and software costs.

ii. It may be difficult for businesses to afford the costs to develop, implement, and maintain AI services.

iii. The protection of sensitive AI information against cybersecurity attacks can also be challenging.

iv. In addition to the need for AI to be adaptable to business needs, significant financial investments may be required for repairs and updates of AI equipment (Bhatia, 2017).

6.4.2 Hidden Costs

As companies prepare for climate change, many fail to observe the critical impact on employee health due to the adverse effects of climate change. This lack of foresight can result in significant financial costs to businesses due to increased healthcare expenses and reduced productivity. Varley (2024) asserted, "Organizations' most valuable assets – their people – face mounting climate-related risks to their physical and mental health from wildfires, extreme heat, hurricanes, flooding, emerging diseases, and more." The hidden costs of climate change on the workforce of the Cayman Islands are significant and multifaceted, impacting not only the economy but also the health and productivity of workers. The following are some of the key hidden costs:

- **Heat Stress:** Extreme heat due to climate change can lead to increased incidents of heat stress among outdoor workers, particularly those in construction, farming, and other manual labour. Such conditions not only reduce productivity but also increase absenteeism and health-related costs. The Cayman Islands, with its tropical climate, is especially vulnerable to these impacts. According to the World Health Organization (WHO), "Productivity losses due to heat stress could amount to a loss of up to 6% of working hours globally by 2030, with tropical regions being the most affected" (WHO, 2019).

- **Vector-Borne Diseases:** The Centers for Disease Control and Prevention (CDC) has noted "an increase in mosquito-borne illnesses in the Caribbean, with climate change contributing to the extended range and breeding season of mosquitoes" (CDC, 2020).

- **Tourism Dependency:** A study by the United Nations Environmental Programme (UNEP) pointed out that "climate change poses a significant risk to Caribbean tourism, with potential revenue losses of up to 25% by 2050 due to declining attractiveness of natural resources" (UNEP, 2022).

- **Climate Change on Employee Health:** The impact of climate change on employee health might be enormous; one estimate found that the direct health costs alone of climate change already far exceed $800 billion per year in the U.S.A. (Varley, 2024). The author further stated that "the importance of timely information cannot be overstated when it comes to climate change and employee health. Just as companies have systems to warn of immediate security threats, similar early warning systems are needed for the growing public health risks linked to climate change" (Varley, 2024).

In summary, it is recommended that further research be conducted on the hidden costs of climate change, especially as it relates to the healthcare of the workforce. The hidden costs of climate change on the workforce in the Cayman Islands are multifaceted, involving direct health impacts, economic instability, and environmental degradation. These costs not only threaten the immediate well-being of workers but also pose long-term risks to the sustainability of the workforce and the overall economy. "Tackling climate change and safeguarding employee health is a major opportunity for today's corporate leaders; these actions not only benefit individual employees but also ease the strain on public health systems and contribute directly to a stronger corporate bottom line. This 'triple win' – employees, the public sector, and businesses – is undeniable" (Varley, 2024). Talia Varley, MD, is the physician lead for Global Corporate Advisory at Cleveland Clinic.

The final thoughts are that while the integration of AI in SIDS, like the Cayman Islands, may prove to be essential for the enhancement and efficiency of businesses, such decisions may also present challenges such as high upfront costs, skill gaps, and ethical concerns. Based on the foregoing advantages and disadvantages of integrating AI into businesses in the Cayman Islands, appropriate strategies must be developed to mitigate the inherent risks while maximizing the benefits of AI adoption.

The regulatory environment for AI is still evolving, and as a result, businesses must navigate complex and changing compliance requirements. It can, therefore, be argued that the most critical decision to be made prior to adopting AI into businesses in SIDS, including the Cayman Islands, is to define clearly the specific benefits that will accrue to the business and that the AI adoption is purposeful and aligned with the strategic goals of the business. This involves understanding the needs and objectives of the business and identifying where AI can provide the most value; such a decision sets the foundation for selecting the right AI tools, planning effective implementation, and ultimately achieving meaningful and measurable results.

The Cayman Islands represent the need for a critical and urgent response to the increasing threats posed by rising sea levels, more frequent and severe hurricanes, and other climate-related challenges. As a small island nation, the Cayman Islands are particularly vulnerable to these global environmental shifts, which threaten both the natural ecosystems and the socio-economic stability of the region. Throughout this book, we have explored the multidimensional aspects of climate resiliency, from infrastructure adaptation and coastal management to sustainable tourism and community engagement. A key takeaway is that resilience planning must be holistic, integrating both immediate mitigation efforts and long-term strategies to build adaptive capacity across all sectors of society. Also, future research is recommended on the hidden costs of climate change, especially as it relates to healthcare.

Effective resiliency planning in the Cayman Islands hinges on the collaboration between government agencies, the private sector, and local communities. Policy frameworks that promote sustainable development, enforce strict building codes, and incentivize renewable energy adoption are foundational to these efforts. Additionally, the incorporation of indigenous knowledge and the active participation of local communities will ensure that strategies are culturally relevant and grounded in the lived realities of the islands' inhabitants. The path forward for the Cayman Islands demands both innovation and commitment. International partnerships and access to climate financing will be essential in bolstering local efforts. Moreover, the experience of the Cayman Islands can serve as a model for other small island nations grappling with similar challenges, fostering a global dialogue on best practices for climate resilience.

Finally, while the challenges posed by climate change are formidable, the Cayman Islands have the opportunity to emerge as leaders in climate resiliency. By prioritizing sustainable development, investing in adaptive infrastructure, and fostering community resilience, the Cayman Islands can safeguard its future against the uncertainties of a changing climate. The journey ahead requires not only strategic foresight but also a shared vision of a resilient and sustainable Cayman Islands for generations to come.

6.5 Recommendations for Research on the Viability of Carbon Capture Storage (CCS) for CO2 Emissions

Should businesses in Small Island Developing States (SIDS) such as the Cayman Islands consider using Carbon Capture Storage (CCS) to dispose of CO2 emissions from large facilities such as power and electricity utilities, cement manufacturing companies, and seawater desalination systems?

For businesses in Small Island Developing States (SIDS) like the Cayman Islands, considering Carbon Capture Storage (CCS) for CO2 emissions involves weighing economic, environmental, and logistical factors. Below is an analysis supported by relevant references and reasoning:

i.   **Economic and Financial Viability**

- **High Costs:** CCS technology is known for its high capital and operational costs, which the relatively small economies of SIDS may not easily support. According to the International Energy Agency (IEA), large-scale CCS projects require substantial initial investments and continuous financial inputs for maintenance and operation (IEA, 2020a). This can be a significant challenge for SIDS, where financial resources are often limited and need to be allocated to other critical infrastructure and resilience projects.

- **External Funding:** To consider CCS, SIDS would likely need external financial support. The Green Climate Fund (GCF) and other international climate finance mechanisms could provide funding for pilot projects, but long-term financial sustainability remains a concern (Green Climate Fund, 2022).

ii. **Geological Suitability**

- **Storage Challenges:** CCS requires specific geological formations for safe, long-term CO2 storage, such as deep saline aquifers or depleted oil and gas fields. The Intergovernmental Panel on Climate Change (IPCC) notes that geological storage must be thoroughly assessed for safety and effectiveness (IPCC Special Report on CCS, 2005). The Cayman Islands, with its small land area and unique geology, may face challenges in finding suitable storage sites that meet international safety standards.

- **Feasibility Studies:** A comprehensive geological assessment would be necessary to determine if local subsurface formations are capable of safely storing CO_2. Without suitable storage sites, CO_2 would need to be transported off-island, which adds complexity and cost.

iii. **Infrastructure and Logistical Barriers**

- **Infrastructure Requirements:** Implementing CCS involves complex infrastructure, including CO_2 capture technology, compression systems, and pipelines or transport facilities for CO_2 movement to storage sites. For a small island like the Cayman Islands, building such infrastructure could disrupt existing land use and strain resources.

- **Technical Expertise:** The deployment of CCS requires skilled personnel for operation and monitoring. SIDS often lack the necessary technical expertise to manage CCS projects, necessitating training or hiring from abroad, which increases operational costs (Global CCS Institute, 2022).

iv. **Alternative Solutions and Energy Strategies**

- **Renewable Energy Potential:** The United Nations Environment Programme (UNEP) emphasizes that renewable energy solutions, such as solar, wind, and geothermal, are more practical for SIDS due to their lower cost, scalability, and suitability for island environments (UNEP, 2020). The Cayman Islands have the potential to harness solar energy and could prioritize this over CCS to reduce CO2 emissions.

- **Energy Efficiency Measures:** Implementing energy efficiency measures in power generation and manufacturing can provide immediate and cost-effective CO2 reductions without the complexities of CCS (IEA, 2020a).

- **Carbon Offsetting and Natural Solutions:** Investment in carbon offset programs, such as reforestation or blue carbon initiatives (mangroves and seagrass restoration), can also provide effective CO2 mitigation while enhancing local ecosystems (Blue Carbon Initiative, 2020).

v.   **Environmental and Community Considerations**

- **Risk of Leakage:** CCS poses risks of CO2 leakage, which could have severe consequences for local ecosystems and communities. The IPCC highlights that while CO2 storage can be secure, monitoring and maintaining the integrity of storage sites is essential (IPCC Special Report on CCS, 2005). For an island community, any accidental release could be especially problematic given the proximity to populated areas and reliance on coastal and marine ecosystems.

- **Community Engagement:** Projects like CCS need significant community buy-in. Public awareness and education on CCS are often limited, and gaining local

73

support may be challenging without clear benefits (Global CCS Institute, 2022).

vi.   Lack of Established Frameworks

Many SIDS, including the Cayman Islands, may not have the regulatory frameworks in place to govern CCS projects. Developing these regulations would require time, resources, and collaboration with international bodies.

Conclusion

Businesses in the Cayman Islands and similar SIDS should carefully evaluate whether CCS is a feasible solution for CO_2 disposal. While CCS can be effective in reducing emissions, the economic, geological, and logistical constraints make it a challenging option for small islands. Instead, focusing on renewable energy integration, energy efficiency, and natural carbon sequestration projects may provide more practical, cost-effective, and sustainable pathways for reducing CO_2 emissions in the region.

Chapter 7: Epilogue

President Trump's Climate Change Policy: Fossil Fuels versus Renewables and its Impacts on Global Climate Change and vulnerability to SIDS such as the Cayman Islands.

Introduction

In view of the potential global threat of President Trump's Climate Change Policy, the following commentary is provided. Climate change remains one of the most pressing and scientifically validated global challenges of the 21st century, with widespread environmental, economic, and social implications. Despite overwhelming scientific consensus on the anthropogenic causes of climate change, former and current U.S. President Donald J. Trump—serving as the 45th (2017-2021) and 47th (2025-present) President—has consistently downplayed its significance. During his terms, Trump labeled climate change a "hoax" and implemented a range of policies that rolled back environmental protections, withdrew the United States from the Paris Agreement, and promoted fossil fuel development at the expense of renewable energy investment (Trump, 2017; UNFCCC, 2020). These positions stand in stark contrast to findings by the IPCC (2021), which concludes with high confidence that human activities—particularly the combustion of fossil fuels—are the primary drivers of global warming. Leading climate scientists warn that continued inaction will lead to irreversible impacts, including rising sea levels, biodiversity loss, extreme weather events, and the displacement of vulnerable populations, particularly in SIDS (IPCC, 2022). The scientific community has categorically rejected claims denying the existence of climate change, underscoring the need for evidence-based policymaking in addressing this existential threat (Vohra, K. *et al.*, 2021).

Scientific Perspectives on Fossil Fuel Policies

1. **Climate Change and Greenhouse Gas Emissions:** The overwhelming scientific consensus is clear: fossil fuel combustion is the dominant source of GHG emissions, particularly carbon dioxide (CO_2), which is the primary driver of anthropogenic global warming (IPCC, 2021). Burning coal, oil, and natural gas releases vast amounts of CO_2, trapping heat in the atmosphere and leading to rising global temperatures, sea-level rise, and extreme weather events.

2. **Health Impacts:** Fossil fuel use contributes significantly to air pollution, which is linked to respiratory diseases, cardiovascular conditions, and premature deaths. A global study found that exposure to particular matter (PM2.5) from fossil fuel combustion accounted for more than 8 million premature deaths worldwide in 2018 (Vohra *et al.*, 2021).

3. **Economic and Social Costs:** While fuels have historically supported industrial growth, the long-term economic costs associated with climate change—such as extreme weather, infrastructure damage, crop failures, and health care expenses—far outweigh their short-term benefits (Stern, 2007). Economists warn that failing to transition away from fossil fuels could result in trillions of dollars in damages by the end of the century.

4. **Environmental and Ecological Damage:** Fossil Fuel extraction methods—such as fracking, coal mining, and offshore drilling—have profound ecological consequences. These include deforestation, habitat destruction, water contamination, and oil

spills (WWF, 2023). In particular, methane leakage from natural gas operations is a significant concern, as methane is over 80 times more potent than CO_2 in the short term (EPA, 2022).

5. **Impact on Vulnerable Populations:** Climate Change caused by fossil fuels disproportionately affects vulnerable populations, including SIDS such as the Cayman Islands, the elderly, low-income communities, and indigenous peoples (IPCC, 2022). Rising sea levels, heatwaves, and extreme weather threaten food security, housing, and access to clean water.

Major Policy Decisions on Climate Change by President Trump

President Trump's climate change policies during his tenures as the 45th (2017-2021) and 47th (2025-present) president of the United States have been characterized by a strong emphasis on promoting fossil fuel industries and rolling back environmental regulations. Trump argued that the Paris Agreement was detrimental to American economic interests, particularly the coal industry, claiming it would cause a significant loss of jobs and hinder industrial growth; his approach to climate change was rooted in skepticism toward the scientific consensus on global warming. President Trump and several key officials frequently questioned the reality and severity of climate change, leading to policy decisions that diverged sharply from prior administrations (Trump, 2017).

Basic overview of President Trump's major climate change policies:

First Term (45th President, 2017-2021)

1. **Withdrawal from the Paris Agreement:** Trump announced the U.S. withdrawal from the Paris Agreement in 2017, claiming it harmed American economic interests (UNFCCC, 2017).

2. **Repeal of the Clean Power Plan:** His administration repealed the Obama-era Clean Power Plan, replacing it with the less restrictive Affordable Clean Energy rule (EIA, 2019).

3. **Rolling Back Over 100 Environmental Regulations:** The Trump administration rolled back key climate and environmental protections, including emissions rules, methane standards, and waterway protections (The New York Times, 2021).

4. **Promotion of Fossil Fuel Infrastructure:** He expanded leasing on federal lands for oil and coal, revived pipeline projects like Keystone XL, and prioritized fossil fuel exports (IEA, 2020b).

Second Term (47th President, 2025-Present)

1. **Second Withdrawal from the Paris Agreement:** On his first day back in office in 2025, Trump signed an executive order to re-exit the Paris Agreement (The Guardian, 2025a).

2. **Declaration of a National Energy Emergency:** Trump declared an energy emergency in early 2025 to expedite fossil fuel projects and streamline environmental reviews (Houston Chronicle, 2025).

3. **Dismantling Environmental Regulations:** The EPA under his second administration began rescinding pollution controls and weakened the National Environmental Policy Act (NEPA) (The Guardian, 2025b; Vox, 2025).

4. **Suspension of Renewable Energy Projects:** Federal support for clean energy projects was paused, and offshore wind permits were blocked (Vox, 2025).

5. **Termination of U.S. Climate Finance Programs:** Trump ended U.S. contributions to international climate finance mechanisms, halting funding to vulnerable developing nations (Health Policy Watch, 2025).

Summary of the U.S. Withdrawal from the Paris Agreement

- **Background:** The Paris Agreement, adopted in 2015, is an international treaty that aims to limit global warming to well below 2°C above pre-industrial levels, with efforts to limit the increase to 1.5°C (UNFCCC, 2015). The United States, under President Barack Obama, was a key player in negotiating and signing the agreement.

- **Trump Administration Withdrawal:** On 1 June 2017, President Trump, serving as the 45th President of the United States, announced that the U.S. would withdraw from the Paris Agreement, citing the need to protect American jobs, sovereignty, and economic interests (Trump, 2017). He argued that the agreement imposed unfair environmental standards on the U.S. while allowing significant emitters like China and India to operate under more lenient terms. The withdrawal officially took effect on 4 November 2020, following the agreement's terms, which required a three-year waiting period and a one-year notice (UNFCCC, 2020).

- **Global and Domestic Reaction:** The decision drew significant international criticism and concern over the loss of U.S. leadership in climate governance. Many domestic stakeholders—including U.S. cities, states, and corporations—committed to upholding the goals of the Paris Agreement independently through the "We Are Still In" coalition (World Resources Institute, 2020).

- **Rejoining Under President Biden:** The United States rejoined the Paris Agreement on 20 January 2021, the first day of President Biden's term. His administration signaled a renewed commitment to climate leadership, reversing Trump's policy (The White House, 2021).

Scientific Prognostications of the Impacts of Climate Change Denial Rhetoric

- Baseless assertions that Climate Change is a "hoax", such as those made repeatedly by President Donald Trump, have serious scientific and societal consequences. The scientific community warns that climate denialism delays urgent mitigation efforts, undermines public trust in science, and fosters policy paralysis (Oreskes and Conway, 2010). Leading climate researchers stress that delaying decarbonization increases the likelihood of surpassing critical climate thresholds—such as 1.5°C of global warming—thereby accelerating sea-level rise, biodiversity collapse, and the frequency of extreme weather events (IPCC, 2021).

- By questioning well-established climate science, such rhetoric erodes public understanding and polarizes environmental discourse. Studies have shown that misinformation and political perceptions of climate risk reduce support for climate policy and impede grassroots mobilization (Lewandowsky, 2019). Moreover, when climate change is dismissed at the highest levels of government, it dampens international cooperation, weakens the enforcement of multilateral agreements like the Paris Accord, and undermines climate justice efforts, especially for vulnerable populations such as SIDS (UNEP, 2022).

- President Trump's opposition to climate change science and his withdrawal from the Paris Agreement have had far-reaching global implications. By undermining international consensus and leadership on climate action, the United States –historically one of the largest greenhouse gas emitters—temporarily removed itself from coordinated global mitigation efforts (UNFCCC, 2020). The weakened momentum for ambitious emission reductions emboldens climate-sceptic leaders and jeopardizes the credibility of multilateral agreements (Oreskes and Conway, 2010). The decision also reduced critical financial and technological support for climate adaptation in vulnerable nations, particularly in the global South and SIDS such as the Cayman Islands, who bear disproportionate impacts of Climate Change despite contributing the least to the GHG problem (UNEP, 2022; IPCC, 2022). Scientific experts warned that the delay in global cooperation resulting from the U.S. withdrawal increases the likelihood of exceeding the 1.5°C warming threshold, thereby accelerating increased numbers and intensity of extreme weather events worldwide (IPCC, 2021). Overall, Trump's stance significantly set back global climate efforts during a critical decade for action.

Executive Summary

Global Impacts of President Trump's Climate Change Opposition

President Trump holds an executive order announcing the U.S. withdrawal from the Paris Agreement on 20 January 2025. This marked the second time the United States retreated from the global climate pact under his leadership, reflecting Trump's continued opposition to climate action.

Introduction

President Donald Trump's stance on climate change—characterized by open denial of climate science and the withdrawal of the United States from the Paris Agreement—has had wide-ranging global impacts. As the 45th U.S. President (2017-2021), Trump famously called climate change a "hoax" and rolled back numerous environmental regulations (Milman, 2024). His administration's decision to quit the Paris Agreement in 2017 (formally completed in 2020) signaled a retreat from international climate cooperation. After retaking office as the 47th President in 2025, Trump once more moved to withdraw the U.S. from the Paris accord, doubling down on policies that ignore scientific warnings and prioritize short-term domestic interests over global climate action (Gibson, 2025). This executive summary analyzes the global implications of Trump's climate-change opposition across four key dimensions: **Scientific, environmental, economic, and diplomatic.**

Scientific Implications

Trump's climate denial rhetoric starkly contradicted scientific consensus. He repeatedly dismissed global warming as "one of the great scams of all time" (Milman, 2024), mocked renewable energy, and even falsely claimed the planet "has actually got a bit cooler recently" (Milman, 2024). By sowing doubt on climate science, his rhetoric undermined public understanding and disregarded the urgency emphasized by experts (Gibson, 2025). Climate scientists warn that delaying action during this critical decade dramatically raises the risk of overshooting the Paris Agreement's central target of limiting warming to 1.5°C. Indeed, Trump's policies have come at a time when global temperatures are hitting concerning milestones—**2024 was the hottest year on record, and the first year that average global temperatures exceeded 1.5°C above prehistoric levels** (Abnett and Furness, 2025). Leading experts cautioned that continued inaction could make stabilizing below 1.5°C impossible (Milman, 2024). For example, climatologist Michael Mann stressed that a second Trump term would be "game over" for meaningful climate progress this decade (Milman, 2024). **In short, scientific prognoses are dire**: Trump's opposition has delayed emissions cuts when the world must "halve emissions by 2030" to avoid catastrophic climate tipping points (Milman, 2025; WMO,2022).

Environmental Impacts

The environmental consequences of Trump's climate stance are global and potentially long-lasting. We are already witnessing escalating climate disasters at roughly 1.1°C of warming – from record heatwaves and wildfires to intensifying hurricanes and droughts (Milman, 2024). Trump's aggressive push to expand fossil fuel extraction ("drill, baby, drill") and roll back pollution limits translates into higher greenhouse gas emissions, further aggravating these trends (Milman, 2024). **One analysis estimated that** Trump's agenda would add several billion tonnes of CO_2 that would not otherwise be emitted, contributing to more frequent floods, fires, and toxic air pollution worldwide (Milman, 2024). This delay in U.S. mitigation efforts inches the planet closer to an "unlivable climate" scenario (Milman, 2024).

Crucially, Trump's policies have a disproportionate impact on vulnerable regions. SIDS and low-lying coastal nations, which contribute only a fraction of global emissions (e.g., Pacific Islands states = 0.02%), are on the frontlines of climate change (Palatino, 2025). By weakening global action, Trump's stance effectively increases the risks of sea-level rise, coral bleaching, and extreme storms for these nations, threatening their very existence. Papua New Guinea's Prime Minister reminded the U.S. of its "moral responsibility" as a top emitter, noting that *"if this planet sinks, we all sink with it"* (Palatino, 2025). Overall, the environmental legacy of Trump's climate opposition is one of exacerbated global risks, potentially locking in more severe long-term damage to ecosystems and communities due to postponed climate action (Gibson, 2025).

Economic Impacts

Trump often justified his climate rollbacks in economic terms, but experts argue that his approach carried significant financial costs and missed opportunities. By exiting the Paris Agreement and scrapping clean energy initiatives, the U.S. forwent leadership in the booming renewable energy sector. Investment in low-carbon industries shifted abroad, as businesses sought a stable pro-climate environment in Europe and Asia (Abnett and Furness, 2025). A coalition of major companies warned that Trump's agenda would "drive green investment elsewhere", allowing other economies to attract the jobs and innovation of the future (Abnett and Furness, 2025). In other words, the U.S. risked ceding its competitive edge in emerging clean technologies (such as solar, wind, and electric vehicles) by clinging to fossil-fuel priorities.

There are also substantial health and climate-related costs associated with Trump's rollbacks. The administration's reversal of pollution standards meant losing significant public health benefits. The Environmental Protection Agency's analysis showed that targeted clean air and water rules would have prevented nearly 200,000 premature deaths in the coming decades and saved hundreds of billions of dollars in health costs (Milman and Noor, 2025). For example, scrapping regulations on power plant and vehicle emissions would increase respiratory and cardiac illnesses, translating to higher healthcare expenses and labor productivity losses (Milman and Noor, 2025). One review found that for every $1 saved by polluters via deregulation, the public bears about $6 in added health costs from problems like asthma, cancer, and heart disease (Milman and Noor, 2025). Moreover, unchecked climate change itself carries hefty economic burdens: more frequent extreme weather events result in costly disaster recovery and infrastructure damage globally. In sum, Trump's climate obstruction undermined the long-term health of the economy, from missed clean energy investments to escalating costs of climate impacts, undercutting the very prosperity and public welfare that leaders are meant to protect (Gibson, 2025).

Diplomatic Impacts

Trump's withdrawal of the U.S. from the Paris Agreement and overall climate skepticism produced a diplomatic rift in global environmental cooperation. The Paris accord, signed by nearly 200 nations, was a landmark of collective effort; America's exit under Trump weakened the multilateral system and eroded trust (Gibson, 2025). Allies and rivals alike were sent the message that the world's largest historical emitter was "abandoning its moral and practical obligations" on climate (Gibson, 2025). This retreat threatened to unravel hard-fought progress and prompted fears that other countries might also waver in their commitments, risking a domino effect of weakened ambition (Milman, 2024). While most nations remain in the agreement, the U.S. absence meant a slashed climate finance for developing countries: upon re-entering office in 2025, Trump *immediately halted* all U.S. payments under U.N. climate agreements, cutting off at least $11 billion pledged to help poorer nations adapt (Abnett and Furness, 2025). This funding gap hit vulnerable nations hard, as those funds were earmarked for resilience-building in communities facing floods, droughts, and other climate disasters (Palatino, 2025). American pullback also left international initiatives like methane reduction and forest conservation with less cooperation from one of the world's top emitters (Milman, 2024).

Diplomatically, the U.S. climate reversal created friction with allies and advantaged geopolitical competitors. The European Union, for instance, forged ahead with its Green Deal and even considered carbon border tariffs on imports – a move that could pit a climate-active EU against a climate-ambivalent America in trade (Milman, 2024). Meanwhile, China and other major emitters could use U.S. inaction as political cover to delay their own cuts, even as climate collaboration between Washington and Beijing ground to a halt under Trump (Milman, 2024). The overall result was a more fragmented global response to climate change at a time when unity is paramount. SIDS, having contributed little to the problem, felt betrayed and urged the U.S. to reconsider its stance, calling Trump's withdrawal a "troubling precedent" with "grave consequences" for international climate efforts (Palatino, 2025). In summary, Trump's approach to climate diplomacy weakened the cooperative spirit of the Paris Agreement, undermined U.S. credibility abroad, and left a leadership void that complicated worldwide efforts to meet our shared climate goals (Gibson, 2025).

In closing, President Trump's withdrawal from the Paris Agreement represents more than a symbolic rejection of international climate cooperation—it has material consequences for the world's most climate-vulnerable nations, such as SIDS, including the Cayman Islands; which face an existential threat from rising sea levels, coral reef degradation, coastal erosion, and more intense tropical storms, all of which are amplified by global warming. By retreating from a framework designed to limit global temperature rise and finance adaptation in developing regions, the United States under President Trump weakened both the momentum and the mechanisms required to support SIDS in managing climate risks (UN-OIHRLLS, 2021). This withdrawal not only delayed global mitigation efforts but also undermined climate justice, as SIDS contribute the least to global emissions, yet suffer the most from their effects. The loss of U.S. leadership and funding during this critical decade has placed nations like the Cayman Islands at greater risk of ecological, economic, and social disruption, deepening inequality in the global response to climate change (UNFCCC, 2020; Palatino, 2025).

References

Abbasi, T., Premalatha, M. and Abbasi, S.A. (2010) 'The return to renewables: Will it help in global warming control?' *Renewable and Sustainable Energy Reviews* 15. Available at: www.elsevier.com/locate/rser (Accessed: 10 February 2024).

Abnett, K. and Furness, V. (2025) *Trump's Paris climate exit will hit harder than in 2017. Reuters, 21 January.* Available at: https://www.reuters.com/sustainability/sustainable-finance-climate-impact-trump-parisexit-2025-01-21 (Accessed: 25 March 2025).

Adger, W.N. *et al.* (2009) 'Are there social limits to adaptation to climate change?' *Springer.* Available at: https://link.springer.com (Accessed: 21 March 2024).

Adger, W.N. *et al.* (2011) 'Resilience implications of policy responses to climate change.' *John Wiley & Sons Ltd.* Available at: https://wires.onlinelibrary.wiley.com/doi/10.1002/wcc.133 (Accessed: 11 February 2024).

Alameldeen, A. and Cakan, Z. (2021) 'What is a Resilient Community?' *Academia Letters.* Available at: https://doi.org/10.20935/AL3615 (Accessed: 15 February 2024).

Argyroudis, S.A., *et al.* (2021) 'Digital technologies can enhance climate resilience of critical infrastructure.' *Climate Risk Management,* 35. Available at: www.elsevier.com/locate/crm (Accessed: 3 March 2024).

Attard, M-C. *et al.* (2021) 'Long-Term Strategies in SIDS: Blueprints for Decarbonised and Resilient 1.5°C

Compatible Economies.' *Impact.* Available at: https://library.sprep.org/sites/default/files/2021-05/long-term-strategies-SIDS-blueprints.pdf (Accessed: 17 February 2024).

Bahinipati, C.S. (2011) 'Economics of Adaptation to Climate Change: Learning from Impact and Vulnerability Literature.' *Madras Institute of Development Studies.* Available at: https://www.mids.ac.in (Accessed: 21 March 2024).

Bang, G., Hovi, J. and Skodvin, T. (2016) 'The Paris Agreement: Short-Term and Long-Term Effectiveness.' *Politics and Governance,* 4(3). Available at: https://www.cogitatiopress.com/politicsandgovernance/article/view/640/427 (Accessed: 10 February 2024).

Bardan, R. (2024) 'NASA Analysis Confirms 2023 as Warmest Year on Record.' *NASA.* Available at: https://www.nasa.gov/news-release/nasa-analysis-confirms-2023-as-warmest-year-on-record/ (Accessed: 22 February 2024).

Baum, N., Maharjan, N. and Langer, S. (2021) 'Building Resilience in Nepal in the Wake of the 2015 Earthquake: Implementation and Evaluation of the BRI-Building Resilience Interventions.' *Academia Letters.* Available at: https://doi.org/10.20935/AL3886 (Accessed: 17 February 2024).

Baxter, P. and Jack, S. (2008) 'Qualitative Case Study Methodology: Study Design and Implementation for Novice Researchers.' *The Qualitative Report,* 13(4). Available at: https://www.nova.edu/ssss/QR/QR13-4/baxter.pdf (Accessed: 20 February 2024).

Behnassi, M. (2014) 'Geostrategic Implications of Climate Change in the Mediterranean.' *IEMed.* Available at: https://www.iemed.org (Accessed: 17 February 2024).

Berkhout, F.G.H., Hertin, J. and Gann, D.M. (2006) 'Learning to adapt: Organizational adaptation to climate change impacts.' *Climate Change* 78(1). Available at: https://research.vu.nl/ws/portalfiles/portal/2132861/Berkhout+et+al.+2006+CC.pd (Accessed: 22 March 2024).

Berrang-Ford, L., Ford, J.D. and Paterson, J. (2010) 'Are we adapting to climate change?' *Global Environmental Change.* Available at: www.elsevier.com/locate/gloenvcha (Accessed: 6 March 2024).

Betzold, C. (2015) 'Adapting to climate change in small island developing states.' *Springer.* Available at: https://link.springer.com (Accessed: 11 February 2024).

Bhatia, S. (2017) 'Artificial Intelligence for Better Climate Governance.' *International Conference on Business, Education, Law and Interdisciplinary Studies.* Available at: https://doi.org/10.15242/DIRPUB.DIRH0617017 (Accessed: 3 March 2024).

Blue Carbon Initiative (2020). 'Harnessing the Power of Coastal Ecosystems for Climate Mitigation.' Available at: https://www.thebluecarboninitiative.org (Accessed: 12 November 2024).

Boutang, J. *et al.* (2020) 'Climate Change Adaptation: Operational Taxonomy and Metrics.' *Sustainability,* 12 p. 7631. Available at: www.mdpi.com/journal/sustainability (Accessed: 16 February 2024).

Braun, V. and Clarke, V. (2021) 'Conceptual and Design Thinking for Thematic Analysis.' *American Psychological*

Association: Qualitative Psychology (9) 1. Available at: https://doi.org/10.1037/qup0000196 (Accessed: 10 April 2024).

Britannica (2024) 'The Cayman Islands.' *Encyclopedia Britannica, Inc.* Available at: https://www.britannica.com/place/Cayman-Islands (Accessed: 11 February 2024).

Bryman, A. and Bell, E. (2011). *Business Research Methods.* 3rd Edition. Oxford: University Press.

Burnett, N. (2023) 'COP28 The United Nations Climate Change Conference.' *House of Commons Library.* Available at: https://commonslibrary.parliament.uk (Accessed: 19 February 2024).

Camarinhas, C. (2020) 'Planning for resilience: an integrated approach to tackle climate change in the Caribbean.' *United Nations Economic Commission for Latin America and the Caribbean LC/CAR/2020/1.* Available at: https://www.academia.edu/43804181/Planning_for_resil ience_an_integrated_approach_to_tackle_climate_chang e_in_the_Caribbean (Accessed: 12 February 2024).

Cayman Islands Government (2022) 'Cayman Islands Climate Change Risk Assessment.' Available at: https://www.gov.ky (Accessed: 15 October 2023).

CDC (2020) 'Climate Change and Vector-Borne Diseases.' Available at: https://www.cdc.gov (Accessed: 18 August 2024).

Coiante, D. and Barra, L. (1996) 'Renewable Energy Capability to Save Carbon Emissions.' *Solar Energy,* 57(6). Available at: https://www.sciencedirect.com (Accessed: 19 February 2024).

Dalby, S. (2020) 'Environmental Security and Climate Change.' *Oxford Research Encyclopedia of International Studies.* Available at: https://oxfordre.com (Accessed: 15 February 2024).

EIA (2019) *Annual energy outlook 2019.* U.S. Energy Information Administration. Available at: https://www.eia.gov/outlooks/aeo/ (Accessed: 24 March 2025).

EPA (2022) *Overview of greenhouse gases: Methane emissions.* United States Environmental Protection Agency. Available at: https://www.epa.gov/ghgemissions/overview-greenhouse-gases (Accessed: 23 March 2025).

Ekstrom, J.A. and Moser, S.C. (2012) 'Institutions As Key Element To Successful Climate Adaptation Processes: Results From The San Francisco Bay Area.' *ResearchGate.* Available at: https://www.researchgate.net (Accessed: 21 March 2024).

Ghoneem, M.Y.M. (2016) 'Planning for Climate Change, Why does it matter?' *Science Direct.* Available at: https://www.sciencedirect.com (Accessed: 15 February 2024).

Gibson, K. (2025) *The Trump Administration's Retreat from Global Climate Leadership.* Center for American Progress, 21 January.. Available at:

shttps://www.americanprogress.org/article/the-trump-administrations-retreat-from-globalclimate-leadership (Accessed: 25 March 2025).

Global CCS Institute (2022). 'CCS in Small Economies: Challenges and Opportunities.' Available at:

https://status22.globalccsinstitute.com (Accessed: 12 November 2024).

Golafshani, N. (2003) 'Understanding Reliability and Validity in Qualitative Research.' *The Qualitative Report* (8) 4. Available at: www.nova.edu/ssss/QR/QR8-4/golafshani.pdf (Accessed: 24 April 2024).

Government of the Cayman Islands (2010) 'Hurricane Ivan Remembered'. Available at: https://reliefweb.int (Accessed: 10 March 2022).

Grant, R. *et al.* (2023) 'Climate adaptation and resilience indices for the Caribbean region: an assessment of four leading indices.' *Climate and Development.* Available at: https://doi.org/10.1080/17565529.2023.2282482 (Accessed: 12 February 2024).

Green Climate Fund (2022) *Home.* Available at: https://www.greenclimate.fund/ (Accessed: 29 January 2025).

Guba, E.G. and Lincoln, Y.S. (1989) 'Fourth Generation Evaluation.' *Sage Publications Inc.* Available at: https://us.sagepub.com (Accessed: 24 April 2024).

Guba, E.G. and Lincoln, Y.S. (1994) 'Competing paradigms in Qualitative Research.' *APA PsycNet.* Available at: https://psycnet.apa.org (Accessed: 24 April 2024).

Hallegatte, S., Rentschler, J. and Rozenberg, J. (2019). *Lifelines: The Resilient Infrastructure Opportunity.* World Bank. Available at:

https://www.researchgate.net/publication/334437080_Li felines_The_Resilient_Infrrastructure_Opportunity (Accessed: 6 March 2024).

Health Policy Watch (2025. *The United States exits the climate fight.* Available at: https://healthpolicy-watch.news/the-united-states-exits-the-climate-fight/ (Accessed: 23 March 2025).

Hoover, L. (2021) '5 Qualitative Research Designs and Research Methods', *Grand Canyon University.* Available at: https://www.gcu.edu (Accessed: 18 April 2024).

Houston Chronicle (2025). *Trump declares energy emergency in boost for Texas oil and gas.* Available at:

https://www.houstonchronicle.com (Accessed: 24 March 2025).

Hunter, J.W. (2005) 'Climate change small island developing states'. *UNFCCC.* Available at: https://unfccc.int/resource/docs/publications/cc_sids.pdf (Accessed: 14 February 2024).

IEA (2020a). 'CCS: Status and Opportunities.' *International Energy Agency.* Available at: www.iea.org (Accessed: 12 November 2024).

IEA (2020b) *World energy outlook 2020.* International Energy Agency. Available at: https://www.iea.org/reports/world-energy-outlook-2020 (Accessed: 24 March 2025).

IPCC (2005). 'IPCC Special Report on Carbon Dioxide Capture and Storage.' Available at: www.ipcc.ch (Accessed: 12 November 2024).

IPCC (2021) *Climate Change 2021: The physical science basis.* Contribution of Working Group I to the Sixth Assessment Report. Available at:

https://www.ipcc.ch/report/ar6/wg1/ (Accessed: 24 March 2025).

IPCC (2022) *Climate change 2022: Impacts, adaptation and vulnerability.* Available at:

https://www.ipcc.ch/report/ar6/wg2/ (Accessed: 24 March 2025).

Jabareen, Y. (2013) 'Planning the resilient city: Concepts and strategies for coping with climate change and environmental risk.' *Elsevier.* Available at: www.elsevier.com/locate/cities (Accessed: 13 February 2024).

Jain, H. *et al.* (2023) 'AI-enabled strategies for climate change adaptation: protecting communities, infrastructure, and businesses from the impacts of climate change.' *Computational Urban Science.* Available at: https://doi.org/10.1007/s43762-023-00100-2 (Accessed: 3 March 2024).

Jayaram, D. (2013) 'Geostrategic Implications of Environmental Change for Island Nations: A Case Study of Indo-Maldivian Equations.' *Air Power Journal* 8(1). Available at:

https://capsindia.org/wp-content/uploads/2022/09/Dhanasree-Jayaram.pdf (Accessed: 15 February 2024).

Johnston, W. and Cooper, A. (2022) 'Small islands and climate change: analysis of adaptation policy in the Cayman

Islands.' *Regional Environmental Change,* 2 *(45).* Available at: https://doi.org/10.1007/s10113-022-01887-2 (Accessed: 12 February 2024).

Jones, L. and Boyd, E. (2011) 'Exploring social barriers to adaptation: Insights from Western Nepal.' *Global Environmental Change.* Available at:

www.elsevier.com/locate/gloenvcha (Accessed: 21 March 2024).

Jorgenson, A.K. *et al.* (2018) 'Social science perspectives on drivers of and responses to global climate change.' *Wiley Wires Climate Change.* Available at:

https://wires.onlinelibrary.wiley.com/doi/pdf/10.1002/wcc.554 (Accessed: 16 February 2024

Karakosta, C. *et al.* (2013) 'Renewable energy and nuclear power towards sustainable development: Characteristics and prospects.' *Renewable and Sustainable Energy Reviews.* Available at: www.elsevier.com/locate/rser (Accessed: 21 February 2024).

Khadka, N.S. (2023) 'COP28: Should India and China benefit from a climate damage fund?' *BBC World Service.* Available at: https://www.bbc.com/news/world-asia-india-67610621 (Accessed: 14 February 2024).

Koeva, D., Kutkarska, R. and Zinoviev, V. (2023) 'High Penetration of Renewable Energy Sources and Power Market Formation for Countries in Energy Transition: Assessment via Price Analysis and Energy Forecasting.' *Energies,* 16 p.7788. Available at:

https://www.mdpi.com/journal/energies (Accessed: 12 February 2024).

Lawrence, J. and Platt, C. (2005) *Paradise Interrupted.* Available at: https://www.ebay.co.uk (Accessed: 14 June 2024).

Lennon, D. (2022) 'A Brief History of Climate Change.' *The Environmental Magazine.* Available at:

https://emagazine.com/a-brief-history-of-climate-change/ (Accessed: 21 February 2024).

Lewandowsky, S. (2019). *Attitudes towards Climate Change are mediated by perceived social norms.* Springer. Available at: https://link.springer.com (Accessed:24 March 2025).

Li, R., Wang, Q. and Li, L. (2023) 'Does renewable energy reduce per capita carbon emissions and per capita ecological footprint? New evidence from 130 countries.' *Energy Strategy Reviews.* Available at:

www.elsevier.com/locate/esr (Accessed: 17 February 2024).

Manuel-Navarrete, D., Pelling, M. and Redclift, M. (2010) 'Critical adaptation to hurricanes in the Mexican Caribbean: Development visions, governance structures, and coping strategies.' *Global Environmental Change.* Available at: www.elsevier.com/locate/gloenvcha (Accessed: 10 February 2024).

Mendelsohn, R. (2012) 'The Economics of Adaptation to Climate Change in Developing Countries.' *World Scientific Publishing Company.* Available at: www.worldscientific.com (Accessed: 21 March 2024).

Merren T. (2005) *Hurricane Ivan Survival Stories.* Jamaica: The Mill Press. ISBN 976-8168-12-9.

Mewes, S. (2018) 'Mitigation, adaptation and resilience.' *Somerset Wildlife Trust.* Available at: www.dlapiper.com (Accessed: 12 February 2024).

Milman, O. (2024). *Five ways a Trump presidency would be disastrous for the climate.* The Guardian, 28 October. Available at: https://www.theguardian.com/us-news/2024/oct/28/donald-trump-climate-change-environment (Accessed: 24 March 2025).

Milman, O. and Noor, D. (2025) *Trump's EPA aims to cut pollution rules projected to save nearly 200,000 lives: "People will be hurt",* The Guardian, 19 March. Available at: https://www.theguardian.com/us-news/2025/mar/19/trump-epa-pollution-regulation-cuts (Accessed: 24 March 2025).

Ministry of Sustainability & Climate Resiliency (2023) 'Cayman Islands Climate Change Policy 2023-2040.' *Cayman Islands Government.* Available at: www.gov.ky/sustainability/climatechangepolicy (Accessed: 13 June 2023).

Ministry of Sustainability & Climate Resiliency (2023) 'Cayman Islands National Energy Policy 2023-2050.' *Cayman Islands Government.* Available at: www.energy.gov.ky (Accessed: 14 October 2023).

Morrow, S.L. (2005) 'Quality and Trustworthiness in Qualitative Research in Counseling Psychology.' *APA PsycNet.* Available at: https://psycnet.apa.org (Accessed: 25 April 2024).

Muellner, N. *et al.* (2021) 'Nuclear energy – The solution to climate change?' *Energy Policy.* Available at:

www.elsevier.com/locate/enpol (Accessed: 20 February 2024).

Munang, R. *et al.* (2013) 'The role of ecosystems services in climate change adaptation and disaster risk reduction.' *SciVerse ScienceDirect.* Available at:

www.sciencedirect.com (Accessed: 6 March 2024).

Mycoo, M.A. (2017) 'Beyond 1.5°C: vulnerabilities and adaptation strategies for Caribbean Small Island Developing States.' *Springer.* Available at: https://doi.org/10.1007/s10113-017-1248-8 (Accessed: 5 March 2024).

Nurse, L. and Moore, R. (2005) 'Adaptation to Global Climate Change: An Urgent Requirement for Small Island Developing States.' *Reciel* 14(2). Available at: https://onlinelibrary.wiley.com (Accessed: 16 February 2024).

Oreskes, N., and Conway, E.M. (2010). *Merchants of doubt: How a handful of scientists obscured the truth on issues from tobacco smoke to global warming.* New York: Bloomsbury Press.

Ortega-Ruiz, G. *et al.* (2022) 'CO2 emissions and causal relationships in the six largest world emitters.' *Renewable and Sustainable Energy Reviews,* 162. Available at: www.elsevier.com/locate/rser (Accessed: 18 February 2024).

Palatino, M. (2025) *Pacific nations react to Trump's order withdrawing the U.S. from the Paris climate agreement,* Global Voices, 27 January. Available at:

https://globalvoices.org/2025/01/27/pacific-nations-react-to-trumps-order-withdrawing-the-us-from-the-paris-climate-agreement (Accessed: 23 March 2025).

Panadés-Estruch, L. (2021) 'Counting duplicates: a critical assessment of the Cayman Islands Response to COVID-19.' *Caribbean Studies.* Available at: https://doi.org/10.4000/etudescaribeennes.22685 (Accessed: 10 March 2024).

Pflüger, F. (2020) 'A new security challenge: The geopolitical implications of climate change.' *Geopolitics & Energy Security.* Available at: https://www.atlanticcouncil.org (Accessed: 18 February 2024).

Phair, D. and Warren, K. (2021) 'Saunders' Research Onion: Explained Simply. Peeling the onion, layer by layer (with examples).' *GradCoach.* Available at: https://gradcoach.com (Accessed: 19 April 2024).

Phuong, L.T.H., Biesbroek, G.R. and Wals, A.E.J. (2017) 'The interplay between social learning and adaptive capacity in climate change adaptation: A systematic review.' *NJAS: Wageningen Journal of Life Sciences.* Available at: https://doi.org/10.1016/j.njas.2017.05.001 (Accessed: 21 March 2024).

Pinnegar, J. *et al.* (2022) 'Cayman Islands Climate Change Evidence Report.' *UK Centre for Ecology & Hydrology.* Available at: https://www.cefas.co.uk

Raiser, K. *et al.* (2020) 'Is the Paris Agreement effective? A systematic map of the evidence. *Environmental Research Letters.* Available at: https://doi.org/10.1088/1748-9326/ab865c (Accessed: 13 February 2024).

Rashid, Y. *et al.* (2019) 'Case Study Method: A Step-by-Step Guide for Business Researchers.' *International Journal of Qualitative Methods*, 18. Available at: www.readcube.com (Accessed: 20 February 2024).

Rashidi-Sabet, S., Madhavaram, S. and Parvatiyar, A. (2022) 'Strategic solutions for the climate change social dilemma: An integrative taxonomy, a systematic review, and research agenda.' *Journal of Business Research.* Available at: www.elsevier.com/locate/business (Accessed: 19 February 2024).

Reid, H. (2023) 'Climate Change Risk Assessment Report.' *Cayman Islands Government.* Available at: https://www.gov.ky/news/press-release-details/climate-change-risk-assessment-report-released (Accessed: 13 February 2024).

Respitawulan, A. and Rahayu, A.Y.S. (2019) 'The Role of Renewable Energy to Reduce Climate Change: Perspective of Policy Content and Context.' *IOP Publishing.* Available at: https://iopscience.iop.org/article/10.1088/1755-1315/328/1/012005/pdf (Accessed: 15 February 2024).

Robinson, S. (2015) 'Climate change adaptation trends in small island developing states.' *Springer.* Available at: https://cdn.serc.carleton.edu/files/getsi/teaching_materials/climate_change/climate_change_adaptation_trends.pdf (Accessed: 11 February 2024).

Saunders, M. and Tosey, P. (2013). 'The Layers of Research Design.' *Rapport.* Available at: https://www.csd.uoc.gr/~hy109/resources/layers.pdf (Accessed: 19 April 2024).

Saunders, M.N.K., Lewis, P. and Thornhill, A. (2019). *Research Methods for Business Students.* 8th Edition. Harlow: Pearson.

Saunders, M.N.K., Lewis, P. and Thornhill, A. (2023) *Research Methods for Business Students.* Ninth Edition. Harlow: Pearson.

Shellenberger, M. (2017) 'The Nuclear Option: Renewables Can't Save the Planet – but Uranium Can.' *Energy and Civilization – MIT Press.* Available at: https://static1.squarespace.com/static/56a45d683b0be33 df885def6/t/5977b765197aea4af2f6fb28/15010179946 61/Shellenberger_final.pdf (Accessed: 14 February 2024).

Sidenko, S. (2023) 'The Importance of Business Resilience: How BRMs Can Build Resilience in Themselves and Their Organizations.' *BRM Institute.* Available at: https://brm.institute/category/brm-philosophy/ (Accessed: 27 March 2024).

Sims, R.E.H. (2004) 'Renewable energy: a response to climate change.' *Solar Energy.* Available at:

www.elsevier.com/locate/solener (Accessed: 15 February 2024).

Snieder, R. and Larner, K. (2009). *The Art of Being a Scientist: A Guide for Graduate Students and their Mentors.* Cambridge: Cambridge University Press.

Stern, N. (2007) *The economics of climate change: The Stern review.* Cambridge: Cambridge University Press.

Sutcliffe, K.M. and Vogus, T.J. (2003) 'Organizing for Resilience,' in Cameron, K.S, Dutton, J.E. and Quinn, R.E. (eds.) *Positive Organizational Scholarship:*

Foundations of a New Discipline. San Francisco: Berrett-Koehler Publishers, Inc. pp. 94-110. Available at: https://www.researchgate.net/publications/235792901 (Accessed: 6 March 2024).

Taramelli, A., Valentini, E. and Sterlacchini, S. (2014) 'A GIS-based approach for hurricane hazard and vulnerability assessment in the Cayman Islands.' *Ocean & Coastal Management.* Available at:

https://dx.doi.org/10.1016/j.ocecoaman.2014.07.021 (Accessed: 12 February 2024).

Taylor, M.S. (2014) 'Can Green Power Save Us from Climate Change?' *Swiss Society of Economics and Statistics,* 150(1). Available at:

https://sjes.springeropen.com/counter/pdf/10.1007/BF0 3399401.pdf (Accessed: 13 February 2024).

Thomas, A. *et al.* (2020) 'Climate Change and Small Island Developing States.' *Annual Review of Environment and Resources.* https://www.annualreviews.org/doi/pdf/10.1146/annure v-environ-012320-083355 (Accessed: 20 February 2024).

Tompkins, E.L. (2005) 'Planning for climate change in small islands: Insights from national hurricane preparedness in the Cayman Islands.' *Global Environmental Change*, 15. Available at: www.sciencedirect.com (Accessed: 14 February 2024).

Tompkins, E.L., and Hurlston L.A. (2005). 'Natural hazards and climate change: What knowledge is transferable?' *Tyndall Centre for Climate Change Research.* Available at: www.tyndall.ac.uk (Accessed: 16 February 2024).

Tompkins, E.L., Hurlston, L.A. and Poortinga, W. (2009) 'Disaster Resilience: Fear, Friends and Foreignness as Determinants of Risk Mitigating Behaviour in Small Islands.' *Sustainability Research Institute.* Available at: https://www.see.leeds.ac.uk/sri (Accessed: 15 February 2024).

Tompkins, E.L., Lemos, M.C. and Boyd, E. (2008) 'A less disastrous disaster: Managing response to climate-driven hazards in the Cayman Islands and NE Brazil.' *Global Environmental Change*, 18(4). Available at: https://dx.doi.org/10.1016/j.gloenvcha.2008.07.010 (Accessed: 12 February 2024).

The Guardian. (2025a). *Trump signs executive order to re-exit Paris climate agreement.* Available at:

https://www.theguardian.com/us-news/2025/jan/20/trump-executive-order-paris-climate-agreement (Accessed: 23 March 2025).

The Guardian. (2025b). *EPA reverses pollution regulations under Trump second term.* Available at:

https://www.theguardian.com/us-news/2025/mar/19/trump-epa-pollution-regulation-cuts (Accessed: 24 March 2025).

The New York Times (2021). *The Trump Administration Rolled Back more than 100 Environmental Rules.* Available at: www.nytimes.com (Accessed: 24 March 2025).

The White House (2021) *United States reenters the Paris Climate Agreement.* Available at:

https://www.whitehouse.gov/briefing-room/statements-releases/2021/01/20/paris-agreement/ (Accessed: 23 March 2025).

Trump, D.J. (2017) *Statement by President Trump on the Paris Climate Accord.* The White House. Available at: https://trumpwhitehouse.archives.gov/briefings-statements/statement-president-trump-paris-climate-accord/ (Accessed: 24 March 2025).

Turrentine, J. (2022) 'What Are the Solutions to Climate Change?' *NRDC.* Available at:

https://www.nrdc.org/stories/what-are-solutions-climate-change#agriculture (Accessed: 19 February 2024).

UNDP (2024) 'Loss and Damage Fund for Developing Countries.' *UNDP.* Available at: www.undp.org (Accessed: 31 March 2024).

UNEP (2007) 'Climate Action.' Available at: www.unep.org (Accessed: 31 March 2024).

UNEP (2020). 'Renewable Energy in Small Island Developing States.' Available at: https://www.unep.org (Accessed: 12 November 2024).

UNEP (2022). *Emissions gap report 2022.* United Nations Environment Programme. Available at:

https://www.unep.org/.resources/emissions-gap-report-2022 (Accessed: 24 March 2025).

UNESCO (1992) 'Small Island Developing States.' Available at: https://whc.unesco.org/en/sids/ (Accessed: 18 March 2024).

UNFCCC (2015) *The Paris Agreement.* United Nations Framework Convention on Climate Change. Available at:

https://unfccc.int/process-and-meetings/the-paris-agreement/the-paris-agreement (Accessed: 23 March 2025)

UNFCCC (2017) *Statement on the U.S. Decision to withdraw from the Paris Agreement.* Available at: https://unfccc.int (Accessed: 23 March 2025)

UNFCCC (2020) *Status of the U.S. withdrawal from the Paris Agreement.* United Nations Framework Convention on Climate Change. Available at: https://unfccc.int/news/us-formally-exits-paris-agreement (Accessed: 24 March 2025).

UN-OHRLLS (2021) *Small Island Developing States: Challenges in achieving sustainable development.* United Nations Office of the High Representative for the Least Developed Countries, Landlocked Developing Countries and Small Island Developing States. Available at: https://www.un.org/ohrlls/content/small-island-developing-states (Accessed: 24 March 2025).

Varley, T. (2024) 'The Hidden Costs of Climate Change on the Workforce.' *Harvard Business Review.* Available at: https://store.hbr.org (Accessed: 15 August 2024).

Vohra, K. *et al.*, (2021) 'Global mortality from outdoor fine particle pollution generated by fossil fuel combustion: Results from GEOS-Chem', *Environmental Research*, 195, p. 110754, doi:10.1016/j.envres.2021.110754.

Vox. (2025). *Trump administration halts NEPA reviews, offshore wind projects.* Available at: https://www.vox.comn/future-perfect/396745/trump-nepa-environment-rules-ceq (Accessed: 23 March 2025).

Weir, T. and Kumar, M. (2020) 'Renewable energy can enhance resilience of small islands.' *Springer.* Available at: https://doi.org/10.1007/s11069-020-04266-4 (Accessed: 31 January 2024).

Whittaker, J. (2024) 'Report: Extensive beach nourishment needed to save Seven Mile.' *Cayman Compass,* 19 March. Available at: https://www.caymancompass.com (Accessed: 19 March 2024).

WHO (2019) 'Global Heat Stress and Workforce Productivity.' *WHO.* Available at: https://www.who.int (Accessed: 19 August 2024).

World Meteorological Organization (WMO) (2022) *"Now or never" on 1.5°C warming limit – WMO,* WMO Press Release, 4 April. Available at:

https://public.wmo.int/en/media/press-release/now-or-nver-15%c2%B0c-warmimg-limit-wmo (Accessed: 25 March 2025)

World Resources Institute (2020). *We are Still In: Climate action from U.S. cities, states and businesses.* Available at: https://www.wri.org/news/we-are-still-in-climate-action (Accessed: 23 March 2025).

Worth, K. (2023) 'COP28 Agreement Signals "Beginning of the End" of the Fossil Fuel Era.' *UN Climate Press Release.* Available at: https://unfccc.int/ (Accessed: 15 February 2024).

WWF. (2023) *The environmental impact of fossil fuels.* Wildlife Fund. Available at:

https://www.worldlife.org/threats/pollution-from-fossil-fuels (Accessed: 23 March 2025).

Zohuri, B., Moghaddam, M. and Mossavar-Rahmani, F. (2022) 'Business Resilience System Integrated Artificial Intelligence System.' *International Journal of Theoretical & Computational Physics,* 3(1). Available at: www.unisciencepub.com (Accessed: 3 March 2024).

Appendix 1

Whittaker (2024)

A significant amount of sand has been permanently lost from the beach system, the report states.

Laguna Del Mar, on the southern end of Seven Mile Beach, has suffered damage in recent storms.

Appendix 2

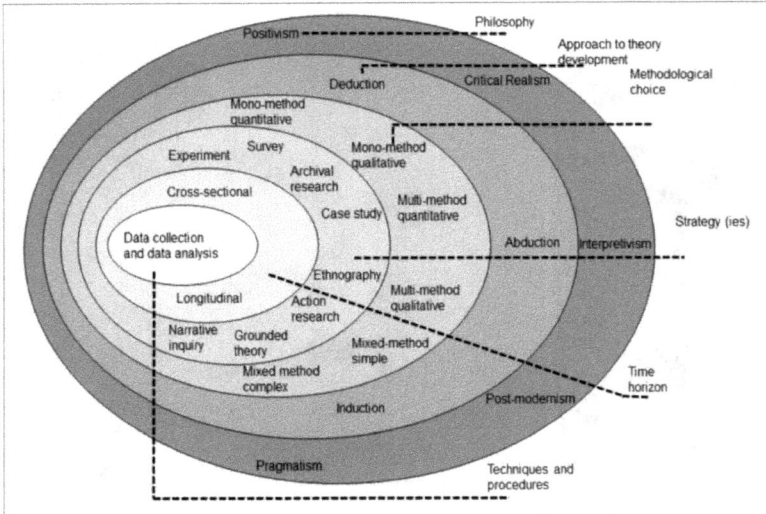

Research Onion (Saunders, Lewis, and Thornhill, 2019, p. 108)

Appendix 3

Interview Questions Relating to the Successful Integration of Climate Change Resiliency Planning Into Businesses in the Cayman Islands

1. Given your experience of the catastrophic damage caused by Hurricane Ivan and/or by the COVID-19 pandemic, what measures have been taken to strengthen the resiliency of your business?

2. What are your perspectives regarding the ability of the Cayman Islands Climate Change Policy (2023-2040) to promote and sustain the integration of climate change resilience into business strategies over these 17 years?

3. What specific resilience and adaptation measures has your business implemented to cope with extreme climate change, such as the rise in sea levels, flooding, and hurricane-force winds?

4. What innovative practices or technologies has your business adopted to enhance climate change resiliency and sustainability?

5. Does your business prioritize and allocate protective measures to integrate resiliency into your business operations successfully? Also, in view of the importance of buy-in by management and staff, has your business experienced resistance to the implementation of climate change resiliency measures? If so, please explain.

Participant's Name & Code:

_____

Participant's Signature: _____

Date:_____

Researcher's Name: Dr. the Hon. Linford A. Pierson, OBE, JP, PhD, LLM, FCCA

Researcher's Signature: _____

Date: _____

Appendix 4

Consent Form for Participation in Research Relating to the Integration of Climate Change Resiliency Into Businesses in the Cayman Islands

Researcher: Dr. the Hon. Linford A. Pierson, OBE, JP, PhD, LLM, FCCA.

P.O. Box 355, Grand Cayman KY1-1106

Phone Number: 345-916-0898

Introduction

You are invited to participate in a research study about how businesses in the Cayman Islands are integrating climate change resiliency planning into their operations. Before you decide whether you wish to participate, you need to understand why the research is being conducted and what it will involve. Please take the time to read the following information carefully.

Purpose of the Study

This study will be used to prepare my dissertation in partial fulfillment of the requirements for the Degree of Master of Business Administration from the University of Cumbria, United Kingdom. This study aims to explore the strategies and practices that businesses in the Cayman Islands are implementing to enhance their resilience to climate change. Your participation will provide valuable insights into effective practices and challenges in integrating climate resiliency planning.

What Does Participation Involve?

If you agree to participate, you will be asked to take part in a face-to-face interview, which will last approximately 30 minutes. During the interview, you will be asked questions about your business's approach to climate change resilience, strategies you have implemented, and your views on the effectiveness of these strategies.

Risks and Benefits

There are no significant risks associated with your participation in this study. While there are no immediate benefits to participants, your contribution will be crucial in understanding and enhancing climate resilience strategies for businesses in the Cayman Islands.

Confidentiality

Your responses will be confidential. The records of this study will be kept private by storing them in an environment with controlled access and will not include any information that can be used to identify you. The data will be summarized and reported in aggregate form in the dissertation and any publications or presentations resulting from this research.

Voluntary Participation

Your participation in this study is entirely voluntary. It is up to you to decide whether or not to take part in this study. If you choose to take part, you will be asked to sign this consent form. You are free to withdraw at any time without giving a reason and without any adverse effects.

Consent:

- I have read and understood the information provided above.

- I have had the opportunity to ask questions, and all my questions have been answered to my satisfaction.

- I understand that my participation is voluntary and that I am free to withdraw at any time without giving a reason and without consequence.

- I agree to take part in this study.

Participant's Name & Code:

_____

Participant's Signature: _____

Date: _____

Researcher's Signature: _____

Date: _____

Please keep a copy of this consent form for your records. If you have any further questions about your participation in this study, feel free to contact the researcher using the contact information provided above.

Alphabetical Codes (A-J) used for Confidentiality of the 10 Participants.

Appendix 5

Photograph taken from Merren (2005)

Foster's Food Fair, Produce Department, after Ivan

Picture by Robert Joseph

Harricane Ivan dealt a severe blow to the chain of Foster's Food Fair stores, all of which received extensive damage. Foster's store at the airport location was flooded and lost its roof, resulting in complete destruction and stranding members of the Foster family who had chosen to shelter there.

Despite all of this, on Tuesday, 14th September 2004, Foster's opened its warehouse and gave away supplies to thousands of people lined up outside the store. All of their stores were flooded with seawater and sewage. In the weeks following the hurricane, the Foster family continued to feed their employees and their families. They also donated thousands of dollars to Cayman's National Recovery Fund, which were applied to building schoolrooms on the island.

www.ingramcontent.com/pod-product-compliance
Lightning Source LLC
Chambersburg PA
CBHW070925270326
41927CB00011B/2724